HOME
TAKEAWAY

HOME TAKEAWAY

COLLINS & BROWN

The Good Housekeeping website is
www.goodhousekeeping.co.uk

ISBN 978-1-909397-55-2

A catalogue record for this book is available from
the British Library.

Reproduction by Mission Productions Ltd,
Hong Kong
Printed and bound by 1010 Printing International Ltd,
China

This book can be ordered direct from the publisher.
Contact the marketing department, but try your
bookshop first.

www.anovabooks.com

NOTES

Both metric and imperial measures are given for
the recipes. Follow either set of measures, not a
mixture of both, as they are not interchangeable.

All spoon measures are level.
1 tsp = 5ml spoon; 1 tbsp = 15ml spoon.

Ovens and grills must be preheated to the specified
temperature.

Medium eggs should be used except where
otherwise specified. Free-range eggs are
recommended.

Note that some recipes contain raw or lightly
cooked eggs. The young, elderly, pregnant women
and anyone with an immune-deficiency disease
should avoid these because of the slight risk
of salmonella.

Contents

Sizzling Street Food

Tandoori Chicken Pittas

Hands-on time: 20 minutes
Cooking time: about 15 minutes

75g (3oz) low-fat yogurt, plus extra to serve (optional)

3 tbsp tandoori paste

1 tsp cornflour

4 skinless chicken breasts

vegetable oil to grease

salt and freshly ground black pepper

To serve

4 wholemeal pitta breads

¼ shredded iceberg lettuce

2 tomatoes, sliced

a large handful of fresh coriander leaves

1 lemon, cut into wedges

mango chutney or natural yogurt (optional)

1 In a large bowl, stir together the yogurt, tandoori paste, cornflour and some seasoning. Add the chicken and stir to coat.

2 Heat an oiled griddle pan over a medium heat and cook the chicken for 15 minutes, turning once until cooked through.

3 Meanwhile, toast the pittas and split in half. Slice the cooked chicken breasts on an angle. Stuff the pittas with the chicken, lettuce, tomatoes and coriander. Serve with lemon wedges and mango chutney or yogurt, if you like.

Chicken Tarragon Burgers

Hands-on time: 20 minutes, plus chilling
Cooking time: 12 minutes

225g (8oz) minced chicken

2 shallots, finely chopped

1 tbsp freshly chopped tarragon

25g (1oz) fresh breadcrumbs

1 large egg yolk

vegetable oil

salt and freshly ground black pepper

toasted burger buns, mayonnaise or Greek yogurt, salad leaves and tomato salad to serve

1 Put the chicken into a bowl with the shallots, tarragon, breadcrumbs and egg yolk. Mix well, then beat in about 75ml (2½fl oz) cold water and season with salt and ground black pepper.

2 Lightly oil a foil-lined baking sheet. Divide the chicken mixture into two portions and put on the foil. Using the back of a wet spoon, flatten each portion to a thickness of 2.5cm (1in). Cover and chill for 30 minutes.

3 Preheat the barbecue or grill. If cooking on the barbecue, lift the burgers straight on to the grill rack; if cooking under the grill, slide the baking sheet under the grill. Cook the burgers for 5–6 minutes on each side until they are cooked through, then serve in a toasted burger bun with a dollop of mayonnaise or Greek yogurt, a few salad leaves and tomato salad.

Serves 2

Moroccan Lamb Burgers

Hands-on time: 20 minutes
Cooking time: about 20 minutes

1 tsp ground cumin

½ tbsp coriander seeds

1 fat garlic clove

600g (1lb 5oz) lamb mince

finely grated zest of ½ orange

50g (2oz) ready to eat dried apricots,
   finely chopped

½ tbsp vegetable oil

salt and freshly ground black pepper

To serve

100g (3½oz) natural yogurt

½–1 tsp harissa paste, to taste

2 tbsp freshly chopped mint

a large handful of watercress

4 flour tortillas or white khobez wraps

1 In a pestle and mortar, pound the cumin, coriander, garlic and plenty of seasoning until fairly smooth. Scrape into a large bowl and stir in the lamb mince, orange zest and apricots. Divide the mixture equally into four and shape each portion into a flattened patty.

2 Heat the oil in a frying pan over a medium heat and cook for 15–18 minutes, turning occasionally, until cooked through.

3 Meanwhile, in a small bowl, stir together the yogurt, harissa, mint and some seasoning. Serve the burgers and watercress wrapped in the tortillas or wraps, drizzled with the harissa sauce.

Spiced Lamb Kebabs with Crunchy Coleslaw

Hands-on time: 10 minutes
Cooking time: about 15 minutes

1 red onion

1 garlic clove, roughly chopped

1 tsp each ground cumin, coriander and cayenne pepper

350g (12oz) lean lamb mince

a small handful of fresh mint, roughly chopped

½ small red cabbage, finely shredded

150g (5oz) low-fat natural yogurt

juice of ½ lemon

1 tbsp tahini

4 pitta breads (see page 118)

2 large tomatoes, sliced

salt and freshly ground black pepper

1. Preheat the grill to medium. Chop half the onion and put into a food processor with the garlic, spices, lamb mince and most of the mint. Season well and whiz until combined. Divide the mixture into eight and form each piece into a patty. Transfer the patties to a non-stick baking tray and grill for 10–12 minutes, turning once, until cooked through.

2. Finely slice the remaining onion and put into a large bowl with the shredded cabbage. In a small bowl, whisk together the yogurt, lemon juice, tahini and remaining mint. Stir half the yogurt dressing through the cabbage mixture and check the seasoning.

3. Toast the pittas and cut horizontally through the middle to make pockets. Bring the pittas, patties, tomatoes, coleslaw and remaining dressing to the table and let people tuck in.

14

Serves 4

Beef Quesadillas

Hands-on time: 20 minutes
Cooking time: about 45 minutes

½ tbsp vegetable oil

5 spring onions, finely sliced

400g (14oz) lean beef mince

few dashes Tabasco

¼ tsp paprika

1 garlic clove, finely sliced

2 × 400g cans chopped tomatoes

8 flour tortillas

125g (4oz) mature Cheddar, grated

a large handful of fresh coriander,
  roughly chopped

salt and freshly ground black pepper

lime wedges and soured cream to serve

1 Heat the oil in a large frying pan, add the spring onions and fry for 3–5 minutes until just softened. Empty into a large bowl. Over a high heat, brown the beef for 5 minutes until cooked through. Stir in the Tabasco, paprika and garlic and cook for 1 minute. Add the tomatoes and some seasoning and simmer for 10 minutes. Tip the beef mixture into the bowl with the spring onions.

2 Wipe the pan clean, then put back on to a medium heat. Put a tortilla in the pan, then spoon over a quarter each of the beef mixture, cheese and coriander. Top with another tortilla and heat through for 3 minutes.

3 Using a spatula, flip the quesadilla and cook on the other side for 3 minutes. Slide on to a board, then cover with foil. Repeat with remaining tortillas. Serve quartered, with lime wedges and soured cream.

Serves 4

Giant Prawn Spring Rolls

Hands-on time: 25 minutes
Cooking time: about 40 minutes

1 tbsp vegetable oil, plus extra to brush
1 tsp Chinese five-spice powder
1 onion, thinly sliced
250g (9oz) mushrooms, sliced
2 small carrots, cut into thin strips
¼ Savoy cabbage, finely shredded
3 tbsp soy sauce
2 tsp cornflour
2 tbsp oyster sauce
200g (7oz) cooked prawns
100g (3½oz) bean sprouts
8 sheets filo pastry, 350g (12oz)
    total weight
2 tsp sesame seeds
1 tbsp honey
steamed vegetables or boiled rice to
    serve (optional)

1 Heat the oil in a large frying pan or wok over a medium heat and fry the five-spice powder for 10 seconds, then add the onion and cook for 5 minutes until lightly coloured and starting to soften (add a little water if the pan looks too dry). Add the mushrooms and cook for 8 minutes, then stir in the carrots and cabbage and fry for a further 3 minutes.

2 Meanwhile, in a small bowl, stir together 1 tbsp soy sauce with the cornflour to make a paste, then stir in the oyster sauce. Add the mixture to the vegetable pan with the cooked prawns and bean sprouts. Cook for 1 minute, then tip the mixture into a large roasting tin or tray and spread out to cool.

3 Preheat the oven to 200°C (180°C fan oven) mark 6. Keeping any filo you're not working with covered to stop it from drying out, brush a sheet of filo with some of the remaining oil, then fold the sheet in half to make a square. Put an eighth of the filling in a thick line along the left edge, leaving a 4cm (1½in) space above and below the top and bottom of the filling. Fold the top and bottom edges of the pastry over the filling, then roll the filling up in the pastry.

Put on to a non-stick baking tray (seam down), brush with a little more oil and sprinkle over a few sesame seeds. Repeat the process with the remaining squares of filo pastry and filling.

4 Cook the spring rolls for 15–20 minutes until golden. Combine the remaining soy sauce with the honey, 1 tbsp water and the remaining sesame seeds to make a dipping sauce. Serve the rolls with the dipping sauce and steamed vegetables or rice.

FREEZE AHEAD

To make ahead and freeze, prepare the spring rolls to the end of step 3, putting them on a non-stick baking tray. Wrap the whole tray well with clingfilm, then freeze for up to 2 months. To serve, unwrap the tray and complete the recipe, cooking the spring rolls from frozen in the preheated oven for 25–30 minutes until golden brown and piping hot all the way through.

Makes 8

Falafel Pittas

Hands-on time: 20 minutes
Cooking time: about 20 minutes

vegetable oil to shallow-fry

1 onion, chopped

2 garlic cloves, crushed

2 × 400g cans chickpeas, drained
    and rinsed

1 tsp ground cumin

½ tsp dried chilli flakes

a small handful of fresh parsley,
    finely chopped

75g (3oz) ready to eat dried apricots,
    finely chopped

1 large egg, lightly beaten

100g (3½oz) plain flour

salt and freshly ground black pepper

For the sauce

125g (4oz) natural yogurt

2 tbsp freshly chopped mint

finely grated zest of ½ lemon

To serve

pitta breads, toasted (see page 118)

houmous (see page 116)

salad

1 Heat 1 tbsp oil in a large deep-sided pan, add the onion and gently fry for 10 minutes until softened. Add the garlic and cook for 1 minute. Tip into a food processor (put the pan to one side to use later) and add the chickpeas, cumin, chilli, parsley and lots of seasoning. Pulse until the mixture is fairly combined but retaining some texture.

2 Empty the mixture into a bowl and stir in the apricots, egg and flour.

3 Pour enough oil into the empty pan so it comes 3cm (1¼in) up the sides and heat for a few minutes. Pinch off golfball-size pieces of the chickpea mixture and squeeze into balls, then carefully drop into the hot oil (it should sizzle). Working quickly, repeat until the pan is fairly full. Turn the falafels when golden on one side and continue frying until golden on the other side.

4 Using a slotted spoon, lift the falafels out on to kitchen paper and continue the frying process with any remaining mixture.
5 Meanwhile, stir together the sauce ingredients and some seasoning.
6 Serve the falafels with pittas, the sauce, houmous and salad.

SAVE TIME

To get ahead, make these up to a day in advance. Cool completely, then store in an airtight container in the fridge. Reheat in the microwave for 15-second bursts until piping hot (or warm in a preheated hot oven).

Serves 4

Skinny Bean Tacos

Hands-on time: 15 minutes
Cooking time: about 10 minutes

2 × 400g cans chopped tomatoes

2 tsp runny honey

410g can cannellini beans, drained
and rinsed

400g can kidney beans, drained
and rinsed

198g can sweetcorn, drained

1 red onion, finely chopped

salt and freshly ground black pepper

To serve

8 corn tacos

reduced-fat guacamole

a large handful of fresh parsley
leaves, chopped

1 Put the tomatoes into a medium
pan with the honey and plenty of
seasoning. Bring to the boil, then
reduce the heat and simmer until
thickened – about 8 minutes.

2 Stir in both types of beans, the
sweetcorn, onion and some seasoning.
Heat through and check the seasoning.

3 Warm the taco shells according to the
pack instructions.

4 Put the bean mixture, tacos,
guacamole and parsley into separate
bowls, take to the table and let
everyone serve themselves.

Serves 4

Friday Night
Favourites

Chicken Tikka Masala

Hands-on time: 20 minutes
Cooking time: about 30 minutes

1 tbsp vegetable oil

1 large onion, finely sliced

2 tbsp tikka masala paste

2 tbsp tomato purée

500g (1lb 2oz) skinless chicken breasts, cut into bite-size pieces

400g can chopped tomatoes

2 tbsp mango chutney

100ml (3½fl oz) natural yogurt

100ml (3½fl oz) double cream

salt and freshly ground black pepper

large handful fresh coriander, roughly chopped, to garnish

rice or Garlic and Coriander Naans (see page 132) to serve

1 Heat the oil in a large pan (that has a tightly fitted lid). Add the onion and a pinch of salt and cook over a low heat, covered, for 20 minutes or until the onions are completely softened.

2 Take off the lid and stir in the tikka masala paste, tomato purée and chicken pieces. Fry for a few minutes, then add the tomatoes. Bring to the boil, reduce the heat and simmer for 8–10 minutes until the chicken is cooked through.

3 Stir in the chutney, yogurt and cream and heat through. Check the seasoning. Garnish with coriander and serve with rice or Garlic and Coriander Naans, if you like.

Serves 4

Piri Piri Chicken

Hands-on time: 15 minutes
Cooking time: about 45 minutes

1 red onion, cut into 8 wedges

1 tbsp olive oil

4 skinless chicken breasts

1 each red and yellow pepper, seeded and cut into strips

a large handful of fresh coriander or parsley, roughly chopped, to garnish

boiled rice, custy bread or green salad to serve

For the sauce

1 red onion, roughly chopped

2 garlic cloves, roughly chopped

1 red chilli, seeded and roughly chopped (see page 80)

½ tsp smoked paprika

juice of 1 lemon

1 tbsp white wine vinegar

1 tbsp Worcestershire sauce

salt and freshly ground black pepper

1 Preheat the oven to 200°C (180°C fan oven) mark 6. Put the onion wedges into a medium roasting tin or ovenproof serving dish (just large enough to hold the chicken breasts in a single layer), add the oil and toss through. Put into the oven to roast for 15 minutes.

2 While the onions are roasting, make the sauce. Put all the ingredients into a blender and whiz until smooth. Put to one side.

3 Slash the top of each chicken breast to allow the flavours to penetrate. Carefully take the onion tin out of the oven, then add the chicken, sauce and peppers and gently toss everything together to mix. Rearrange the chicken in the tin, cut side up.

4 Cook for 25–30 minutes until the chicken is cooked through. Garnish with coriander or parsley and serve with rice, crusty bread or green salad.

Serves 4

Fish, Chips and Mashed Peas

Hands-on time: 15 minutes
Cooking time: about 40 minutes

4 large baking potatoes, about 900g (2lb)

3 tbsp vegetable oil

25g (1oz) plain flour

1 large egg, beaten

100g (3½oz) fresh white breadcrumbs

4 × 125g (4oz) cod fillets, skinned

450g (1lb) fresh or frozen peas

1½ tbsp finely sliced fresh mint

salt and freshly ground black pepper

tartare sauce, lemon wedges and malt
   vinegar to serve

1 Preheat the oven to 200°C (180°C fan oven) mark 6. Cut the potatoes into wedges and put on a large baking tray. Drizzle with 1½ tbsp of the oil, season well and toss to coat the wedges. Cook in the oven for 30–40 minutes until tender and golden brown.

2 Put the flour, egg and breadcrumbs on to three separate lipped plates.

3 When the wedges are 10 minutes away from being finished, bring a medium pan of water to the boil. Meanwhile, coat each fish fillet in flour, tapping off the excess, then dip into the egg and then into the breadcrumbs.

4 Heat the remaining 1½ tbsp oil in a large, non-stick frying pan and cook the fish for 5 minutes, turning once, or until golden brown and cooked through.

5 Add the peas to the boiling water and cook for 2–3 minutes until tender. Drain. Using a potato masher, roughly crush the peas, then stir in the mint and seasoning to taste. Serve the fish immediately with a dollop of tartare sauce and a lemon wedge, plus the potato wedges and peas, and malt vinegar to sprinkle over.

SAVE MONEY

Frozen fish fillets keep costs down. It's best to thaw them fully before using – in the fridge on a baking tray lined with lots of kitchen paper.

Serves 4

Perfect Pizza

Pizza Base Dough

Hands-on time: 5 minutes, plus rising

Makes: 1 large or 2 small pizza bases

You will need 225g (8oz) strong white bread flour, plus extra to dust, ½ tsp sea salt, ½ tsp fast-action (easy-blend) dried yeast, 1 tbsp extra virgin olive oil, plus extra to grease.

1 Sift the flour and salt into a bowl and stir in the dried yeast. Make a well in the centre and gradually work in 150ml (¼ pint) warm water and the oil to form a soft dough.

2 Turn the pizza dough on to a lightly floured worksurface and knead well for 8–10 minutes until smooth and elastic. (Alternatively, knead the dough in a large food mixer fitted with a dough hook.)

3 Put into an oiled bowl, turn the dough once to coat the surface with oil and cover the bowl with clingfilm. Leave to rise in a warm place for 1 hour or until doubled in size.

4 Punch the dough to knock back and shape as required.

3

4

Toppings

Top the pizza with a thin layer of tomato purée, then scatter one or two of the following on top and finish with grated cheese or slices of mozzarella:

- ❑ Bacon or pancetta bits, or slices of prosciutto
- ❑ Rocket leaves
- ❑ Dried chilli flakes
- ❑ Capers
- ❑ Sliced sun-dried tomatoes
- ❑ Pepperoni slices
- ❑ Roasted peppers
- ❑ Artichoke hearts, drained and quartered
- ❑ Sliced mushrooms

Cook the topped pizzas on baking sheets in an oven preheated to 200°C (180°C fan oven) mark 6 for 15–18 minutes until golden.

Variation

If you like, use 15g (½oz) fresh yeast instead of the fast-action (easy-blend) dried yeast. Mix with 2 tbsp of the flour, a pinch of sugar and the warm water. Leave in a warm place for 10 minutes or until frothy, then add to the rest of the flour and salt. Mix to a dough and continue as above.

Perfect Cheese

Probably the best place to buy cheese is from a specialist cheese shop if you are lucky enough to have access to one, otherwise many supermarkets have a fresh cheese counter offering a good variety of farmhouse and factory-made cheeses.

How to choose cheese

Avoid any cheese that has a strong ammonia odour. Hard or semi-hard cheese that has beads of moisture on the surface, or a dry, cracked rind, should be rejected. Semi-soft cheese should yield to gentle pressure and any powdery bloom on the rind should be evenly coloured and slightly moist.

home will dry out the cheese.

Buying pre-packed cheese
If buying pre-packed cheese, check that it does not look sweaty or excessively runny and that it is within the life of its date stamp. If the date is many weeks ahead, it may mean that the cheese is immature; this may not matter if you intend to store it for using when mature.

Buying cheese for vegetarians
Some vegetarians prefer to avoid cheeses that have been produced by the traditional method, because this uses animal-derived rennet; however, most supermarkets and cheese shops now stock an excellent range of vegetarian cheeses, produced using vegetarian rennet. Always check the label when buying.

Cooking with cheese
The less cooking cheese has, the better. Overheating tends to make it tough and indigestible, so always heat the cheese very gently and do not cook longer than is necessary to melt it. Most hard cheeses are excellent for grating and melting.

Storing cheese
The best way to store cheese is to wrap it in waxed paper, then put it into an unsealed plastic food bag or cheese box. Keep in the fridge in the least cold area, away from the freezer compartment. If you have a whole, rinded cheese, cover the cut surface

Family Favourite Pizza

Hands-on time: 30 minutes, plus rising
Cooking time: about 15 minutes

225g (8oz) strong white flour

½ tsp fast-action (easy-blend) dried yeast

1 tbsp extra virgin olive oil, plus extra for greasing

6 tbsp good-quality ready-made pizza sauce

125g ball buffalo mozzarella, drained and torn into pieces

2 heaped tbsp ready-made pesto

salt and freshly ground black pepper

fresh basil and/or oregano leaves to garnish

1 Sift the flour and ½ tsp salt into a large bowl. Stir in the yeast and make a well in the centre. Stir in the oil and about 150ml (5fl oz) hand-hot water to make a soft but not sticky dough.

2 Knead the dough for 10 minutes on a lightly floured worksurface until smooth and elastic. Put in a lightly oiled bowl, cover with a clean teatowel and leave to rise in a warm place for 1 hour.

3 Preheat the oven to 230°C (210°C fan oven) mark 8 and lightly grease two baking sheets. Knock the air out of the dough and divide in half. Roll each half into a 25cm (10in) circle. Transfer to baking sheets.

4 Spread the bases with the pizza sauce, then top with mozzarella and dollops of pesto. Bake for 10–15 minutes until crisp and golden. Garnish with herbs and plenty of ground black pepper.

Serves 4

Pepperoni Pizza

Hands-on time: 25 minutes, plus rising
Cooking time: about 40 minutes

125g (4oz) strong white flour, plus
extra to dust

½ tsp fast-action (easy-blend)
dried yeast

1 tbsp extra virgin olive oil, plus extra
to grease

125g (4oz) mozzarella cheese, torn into
small pieces

70g pack small pepperoni slices

salt and freshly ground black pepper

For the sauce

1 tsp olive oil

½ onion, finely chopped

1 garlic clove, finely chopped

1–2 tsp dried oregano, to taste

2 tbsp tomato purée

400g can chopped tomatoes

1 tsp caster sugar

1 Sift the flour into a medium bowl
and stir in the yeast and ½ tsp salt.
Quickly mix in the oil and 100ml
(3½fl oz) hand-hot water to make a
soft but not sticky dough (adjust with
water/flour as needed). Knead for a
few minutes, then put in a lightly oiled
bowl, cover and leave to rise in a warm
place for 30 minutes.

2 Meanwhile, make the sauce. Heat the
oil in a medium pan, add the onion
and gently fry for 10 minutes. Add
the garlic, oregano and tomato purée
and fry for a few minutes. Stir in the
tomatoes and sugar. Bring to the boil,
then reduce the heat and simmer for
15 minutes, stirring occasionally, until
thick and pulpy. Check the seasoning
and put to one side.

3 Preheat the grill to high and put the
rack 9cm (3½in) away from the heat
source. Tip the dough out on to a
lightly floured worksurface and roll
out to a 30.5cm (12in) circle – you may
need to let it rest for a few minutes

during rolling to get the dough to stretch properly.

4 Dust a large baking sheet with flour and transfer the pizza base on to the sheet. Grill for 1–2 minutes or until browning (it will blister). Flip and grill for a further 1–2 minutes.

5 Remove the baking sheet from the grill and spread the tomato sauce over the base, leaving a border around the edge. Scatter over the mozzarella and pepperoni and grill for 8–10 minutes (making sure the pizza doesn't catch) until golden. Serve immediately.

Makes 1

Chicken Fajitas

Hands-on time: 15 minutes
Cooking time: 10 minutes

4 large flour tortilla wraps

2 tsp oil

1 garlic clove, crushed

½–1 tsp smoked paprika, to taste

2 tbsp tomato purée

1 tsp runny honey

4 cooked skinless chicken breasts,
   cut into finger-size strips

125g (4oz) roasted red peppers from
   a jar, drained and sliced

a large handful of fresh coriander,
   chopped

salt and freshly ground black pepper

To serve (optional)

guacamole

soured cream

grated Cheddar

1 Stack the tortillas, then wrap in foil. Put into the oven, then turn the oven on to 200°C (180°C fan oven) mark 6 (no need to preheat, as you're just warming the tortillas). Alternatively, wrap tortillas in clingfilm and microwave on full power for 30-second bursts until warmed through.

2 Meanwhile, heat the oil in a large frying pan, add the garlic and paprika and fry for 30 seconds, then stir in the tomato purée, honey and 4 tbsp water. Add the chicken and sliced peppers and simmer for 5 minutes until piping hot. Stir in most of the coriander and check the seasoning.

3 Spoon the chicken mixture into a dish and garnish with the remaining coriander. Serve the mixture with the warmed tortillas, the guacamole, soured cream and grated cheese and let everyone tuck in.

Spicy Bean and Tomato Fajitas

Hands-on time: 15 minutes
Cooking time: 25 minutes

2 tbsp sunflower oil

1 onion, sliced

2 garlic cloves, crushed

½ tsp hot chilli powder

1 tsp ground coriander

1 tsp ground cumin

1 tbsp tomato purée

400g can chopped tomatoes

225g can red kidney beans, drained
and rinsed

300g can borlotti beans, drained
and rinsed

300g can flageolet beans, drained
and rinsed

150ml (¼ pint) hot vegetable stock

2 ripe avocados, quartered and chopped

juice of ½ lime

1 tbsp freshly chopped coriander, plus
extra sprigs to garnish

6 ready-made flour tortillas

150ml (5fl oz) soured cream

salt and freshly ground black pepper

lime wedges to serve

1 Heat the oil in a large pan, add the
onion and cook gently for 5 minutes.
Add the garlic and spices and cook
for a further 2 minutes.

2 Add the tomato purée and cook
for 1 minute, then add the tomatoes,
beans and hot stock. Season well
with salt and ground black pepper
and cook for 15 minutes, stirring
occasionally.

3 Put the avocados into a bowl, add the
lime juice and the chopped coriander,
and mash together. Season to taste.

4 To warm the tortillas either wrap them
in foil and heat in the oven at 180°C
(160°C fan oven) mark 4 for 10 minutes,
or put on a plate and microwave on full
power for 45 seconds.

5 Spoon the beans down the centre
of each tortilla. Add a little avocado
and soured cream, then fold the two
sides in so that they overlap. Garnish
with coriander sprigs and serve with
lime wedges.

Serves 6

Beef Burrito

Hands-on time: 25 minutes
Cooking time: about 25 minutes

1 tbsp vegetable oil

1 onion, finely chopped

1 garlic clove, crushed

500g (1lb 2oz) lean beef mince

½–1 tsp smoked paprika, to taste

2 tsp ground coriander

2 tbsp tomato purée

250g pack microwave basmati rice

198g can sweetcorn, drained

4 flour tortillas

salt and freshly ground black pepper

To serve

Refried Beans (see opposite)

guacamole

soured cream

grated Cheddar

1 Heat the oil in a large pan over a medium heat, add the onion and fry for 10 minutes, until softened. Add the garlic and fry for 1 minute. Add the beef mince and fry, stirring to help break up the mince, for about 8 minutes or until well browned.

2 Add the smoked paprika, ground coriander, tomato purée and plenty of seasoning. Fry for 1 minute before adding the rice, sweetcorn and a splash of water. Heat through and check the seasoning.

3 Meanwhile warm the tortillas according to the pack instructions.

4 To serve, spread a large spoonful of the refried beans on to a warmed tortilla before topping with the mince mixture, some guacamole, soured cream and grated cheese. Roll up and enjoy!

To make refried beans

Melt 25g (1oz) butter in a medium pan, add 1 finely chopped small onion and gently fry for 10 minutes until softened. Meanwhile, drain and rinse 2 x 400g cans kidney beans and whiz in a food processor with 200ml (7fl oz) water until smooth. Put to one side. Add 1tsp ground cumin and plenty of salt to the softened onion and fry for 1 minute, then scrape in the bean mixture. Simmer gently for 15 minutes, then stir through 3 tbsp soured cream and check the seasoning. Serve warm.

Serves 4

Perfect Wok

You don't need to buy special equipment to start stir-frying – a large deep-sided frying pan and a spatula will do the job – but a wok is very versatile, with many uses in the kitchen.

Choosing a wok

Traditional steel woks have rounded bottoms, so the food always returns to the centre where the heat is most intense. The deep sides prevent the food from falling out during stir-frying. Most woks now have flattened bottoms, which makes them more stable on modern hobs. Non-stick woks are widely available; they are easy to clean and not prone to rusting.

❑ There are two main styles of wok, one with double handles opposite each other, the other with one long handle. The double-handled wok gets very hot and needs to be handled with oven gloves, although it is slightly more stable if you use it for steaming and braising

❑ A wok with a long single handle is the best choice as it is easier to manipulate when stir-frying

❑ A wok with a diameter of 35.5cm (14in) is most useful for cooking stir-fries for four people

❑ A well-fitting lid is useful if you intend to use your wok for steaming

Wok equipment

Wok spoon A metal utensil with a curved end to match the curve of the wok is useful for stir-frying in a traditional steel wok, but should not be used in non-stick woks – any heatproof spatula will do.

Chopsticks Long wooden chopsticks are great for stir-frying in non-stick woks; they are also useful for separating blocks of noodles as they cook.

Steamers come in various sizes, and may be of pierced metal or bamboo. They can be used in a wok or over a pan of boiling water, covered with a tight-fitting lid.

Trivet or steamer rack A wooden or metal trivet or steamer rack fits inside the wok to keep food above the water level when steaming.

Wok stand A wok stand or ring, which sits on the hob with the wok on top, helps keep the wok stable during steaming or braising.

Strainer A long-handled strainer is useful for scooping food from deep-frying oil, but a slotted spoon could be used instead.

Seasoning a wok

Non-stick woks do not need to be seasoned. Traditional steel woks, designed to withstand high temperatures, can be made practically non-stick by 'seasoning' before you use them for the first time. First scrub the wok in hot water and detergent, then dry thoroughly with kitchen paper. Place it over a low heat, add 2 tbsp groundnut oil and rub this over the entire inner surface with kitchen paper. Keep the wok over a low heat until the oil starts to smoke. Leave to cool for 5 minutes, then rub well with kitchen paper. Add another 2 tbsp oil and repeat the heating process twice more until the kitchen paper wipes clean. The wok is now seasoned. If used regularly it should remain rust-free. After each use, rinse in hot water – but not detergent – and wipe clean with kitchen paper. If you scrub your wok or use detergent you will need to season it again.

Sweet and Sour Pork Stir-fry

Hands-on time: 15 minutes
Cooking time: about 10 minutes

2 tbsp vegetable oil

350g (12oz) pork fillet, cut into finger-size pieces

1 red onion, finely sliced

1 red pepper, seeded and finely sliced

2 carrots, cut into thin strips

3 tbsp sweet chilli sauce

1 tbsp white wine vinegar

220g can pineapple slices, chopped, with 2 tbsp juice put to one side

a large handful of bean sprouts

½ tbsp sesame seeds

a large handful of fresh coriander, roughly chopped

salt and freshly ground black pepper

boiled long-grain rice to serve

1 Heat the oil over a high heat in a large frying pan or wok. Add the pork, onion, red pepper and carrots. Cook for 3–5 minutes, stirring frequently, until the meat is cooked through and the vegetables are softening.

2 Stir in the chilli sauce, vinegar and reserved pineapple juice and bring to the boil, then stir in the pineapple chunks and bean sprouts and heat through.

3 Check the seasoning. Scatter the sesame seeds and coriander over and serve immediately with rice.

Serves 4

Stir-fried Vegetables with Oyster Sauce

Hands-on time: 20 minutes
Cooking time: about 10 minutes

175g (6oz) firm tofu

vegetable oil to shallow- and deep-fry

2 garlic cloves, thinly sliced

1 green pepper, seeded and sliced

225g (8oz) broccoli, cut into small florets

125g (4oz) green beans, trimmed
   and halved

50g (2oz) bean sprouts

50g (2oz) canned straw mushrooms,
   drained

125g (4oz) canned water chestnuts,
   drained

fresh coriander sprigs to garnish

For the sauce

100ml (3½fl oz) vegetable stock

2 tbsp oyster sauce

1 tbsp light soy sauce

2 tsp runny honey

1 tsp cornflour

a pinch of salt

1 First, make the sauce. Put all the ingredients in a blender and blend until smooth. Put to one side.

2 Drain the tofu, pat it dry and cut it into large cubes. Heat the oil in a deep-fryer to 180°C (test by frying a small cube of bread; it should brown in 40 seconds). Add the tofu and deep-fry for 1–2 minutes until golden. Drain on kitchen paper.

3 Heat 2 tbsp oil in a wok or large frying pan, add the garlic and fry for 1 minute. Remove the garlic with a slotted spoon and discard. Add the pepper, broccoli and beans to the oil in the pan and stir-fry for 3 minutes. Add the bean sprouts, mushrooms and water chestnuts and stir-fry for a further 1 minute.

4 Add the tofu and sauce to the pan and simmer, covered, for 3–4 minutes. Garnish with coriander sprigs and serve immediately.

Serves 4

Go East

Asian Storecupboard

Rice and noodles are the staple foods. The following items, used in many Asian dishes, are available in most large supermarkets and Asian food shops.

Spices

Chinese five-spice powder is made from star anise, fennel seeds, cinnamon, cloves and Sichuan pepper. It has a strong liquorice-like flavour and should be used sparingly.

Kaffir lime leaves, used in South-east Asian cooking for their lime-lemon flavour, are glossy leaves used whole but not eaten – rather like bay leaves. Use grated lime zest as a substitute.

Tamarind paste has a delicately sour flavour; use lemon juice as a substitute.

Sauces

Soy sauce – made from fermented soya beans and, usually, wheat – is the most common flavouring in Chinese and South-east Asian cooking. There are light and dark soy sauces; the dark kind is slightly sweeter and tends to darken the food. It will keep indefinitely.

Thai fish sauce is a salty condiment with a distinctive, pungent aroma. It is used in many South-east Asian dishes. You can buy it in most large supermarkets and Asian food stores. It will keep indefinitely.

Thai green curry paste is a blend of spices such as green chillies, coriander and lemongrass. Thai red curry paste contains fresh and dried red chillies and ginger. Once opened, store in a sealed container in the fridge for up to one month.

Chilli sauce is made from fresh red chillies, vinegar, salt and sugar; some versions include other ingredients such as garlic or ginger. Sweet chilli sauce is a useful standby for adding piquancy to all kinds of dishes.

Black bean sauce is made from fermented black beans, salt and ginger. Salty and pungent on its own, it adds richness to many stir-fry dishes.

Yellow bean sauce is a thick, salty, aromatic yellow-brown purée of fermented yellow soya beans, flour and salt.

Hoisin sauce, sometimes called barbecue sauce, is a thick, sweet-spicy red-brown sauce made from mashed soya beans, garlic, chillies and other spices.

Oyster sauce is a smooth brown sauce made from oyster extract, wheat flour and other flavourings. It doesn't taste fishy, but adds a 'meaty' flavour to stir-fries and braises.

Plum sauce, made from plums, ginger, chillies, vinegar and sugar, is traditionally served with duck or as a dip.

Coconut milk

Canned coconut milk is widely available, but if you can't find it, use blocks of creamed coconut or coconut powder, following the pack instructions to make the amount of liquid you need.

Canned vegetables

Bamboo shoots, available sliced or in chunks, they have a mild flavour; rinse before use.

Water chestnuts have a very mild flavour but add a lovely crunch to stir-fried and braised dishes.

Other ingredients

Dried mushrooms feature in some Chinese recipes; they need to be soaked in hot water for 30 minutes before use.

Dried shrimps and dried shrimp paste (blachan) are often used in South-east Asian cooking. The pungent smell becomes milder during cooking and marries with the other ingredients. These are often included in ready-made sauces and spice pastes, and are not suitable for vegetarians.

Mirin is a sweet rice wine from Japan; if you can't find it, use dry or medium sherry instead.

Rice wine is often used in Chinese cooking; if you can't find it, use dry sherry instead.

Rice vinegar is clear and milder than other vinegars. Use white wine vinegar or cider vinegar as a substitute.

Which oil to use?

Groundnut (peanut) oil has a mild flavour and is widely used in China and South-east Asia. It is well suited to stir-frying and deep-frying as it has a high smoke point and can therefore be used at high temperatures.

Vegetable oil may be pure rapeseed oil, or a blend of corn, soya bean, rapeseed or other oils. It usually has a bland flavour and is suitable for stir-frying.

Sesame oil has a distinctive nutty flavour; it is best used in marinades or added as a seasoning to stir-fried dishes just before serving.

Chicken Pasanda

Hands-on time: 20 minutes
Cooking time: about 25 minutes

300g (11oz) basmati and wild
   rice, washed

½ tbsp vegetable oil

1 onion, finely sliced

5 cardamom pods

1 tsp each ground cinnamon
   and turmeric

½ tsp chilli powder

2 garlic cloves

½ tbsp coriander seeds

4 × 125g (4oz) skinless chicken breasts,
   cut into bite-size pieces

2 tbsp tomato purée

500g tub 0% fat Greek yogurt

salt and freshly ground black pepper

To garnish

15g (½oz) flaked almonds, toasted

a large handful of fresh coriander,
   roughly chopped

1 Cook the rice according to the pack instructions. Heat the oil in a large pan, add the onion and gently cook for 10 minutes.

2 Meanwhile, put the cardamom pods into a mortar and break with a pestle. Remove and discard the outer husks. Add the cinnamon, turmeric, chilli, garlic, coriander seeds and plenty of seasoning and bash to as fine a powder as you can.

3 Add the chicken to the onion pan and fry for 8–10 minutes until cooked through. Stir in the spice mix and tomato purée. Cook for 1 minute.

4 Take off the heat and stir in the yogurt – add a little water if the sauce is too thick. Check the seasoning. Garnish with toasted flaked almonds and fresh coriander. Serve with boiled rice.

Serves 4

Fish Curry

Hands-on time: 20 minutes
Cooking time: about 25 minutes

1 tsp vegetable oil

2 onions, finely sliced

5cm (2in) piece fresh root ginger, grated

1 tsp each ground turmeric and coriander

1 tbsp medium curry paste

4 tomatoes, roughly chopped

400ml (13fl oz) fish stock

200g (7oz) raw, peeled king prawns

300g (11oz) white skinless fish, such as cod, haddock, coley or pollock, cut into 2.5cm (1in) cubes

200g (7oz) frozen peas

salt and freshly ground black pepper

boiled rice or crusty bread to serve

1 Heat the oil in a large pan over a low heat. Add the onions and a good pinch of salt, then cover and cook for 15 minutes until completely softened. Stir in the ginger, turmeric, coriander and curry paste. Cook for 1 minute.

2 Stir in the tomatoes and stock and simmer for 5 minutes. Mix in the prawns, fish and peas, then cook for 3–5 minutes (stirring carefully to prevent the fish from breaking up) until the prawns are bright pink and the fish is opaque. Check the seasoning and serve with rice or crusty bread, if you like.

Serves 4

Paneer Curry

Hands-on time: 20 minutes
Cooking time: about 20 minutes

1 tbsp vegetable oil

1 onion, finely sliced

1 garlic clove, crushed

2 tbsp mild curry paste

165ml can coconut milk

300ml (½ pint) vegetable stock

300g (11oz) mix of broccoli and
  cauliflower florets

200g (7oz) frozen peas

150g (5oz) paneer cheese, cubed

a large handful of spinach

salt and freshly ground black pepper

boiled rice to serve

1 Heat the oil in a large pan over a low
  heat. Add the onion and gently cook
  for about 10 minutes until soft. Add
  the garlic and curry paste and cook
  for 1 minute.

2 Stir in the coconut milk and stock.
  Bring to the boil, then reduce the
  heat, add the florets and simmer for 5
  minutes, until nearly cooked through.

3 Add the peas and paneer, season
  and heat through. Fold through the
  spinach and serve with rice.

Serves 4

Butter Bean Masala

Hands-on time: about 10 minutes
Cooking time: about 10 minutes

½ tbsp vegetable oil

1 shallot, sliced

1 garlic clove, crushed

1 tsp garam masala

¼–½ red chilli (depending on taste – freeze the remainder to use at a later date), seeded and finely chopped

2 tomatoes, roughly chopped

410g can butter beans, drained and rinsed

a handful of fresh coriander or spinach, chopped

salt and freshly ground black pepper

1 Heat the oil in a pan, add the shallot and gently cook for 5 minutes. Stir in the garlic, garam masala and chilli and cook for 1 minute, then add the tomatoes and 100ml (3½fl oz) water. Simmer for 3 minutes, occasionally squashing the tomatoes with a wooden spoon.

2 Stir in the butter beans and heat through. Stir through the coriander or spinach and check the seasoning. Serve immediately.

Serves 1

Simple Seafood Sushi

Hands-on time: 20 minutes
Cooking time: about 15 minutes, plus cooling and chilling

150g (5oz) shortgrain rice, unwashed

100g (3½oz) white crab meat

100g (3½oz) small cooked prawns, finely chopped

1 avocado, stoned and finely chopped

1 red pepper, seeded and finely chopped

2 tbsp extra light mayonnaise

2 tbsp rice wine mirin

½ tbsp sesame seeds

4 sheets dried seaweed, each approx. 19cm × 22cm (7½in × 8½in)

To serve

pickled ginger (optional)

wasabi (optional)

soy sauce (optional)

green salad

1 Put the unwashed rice in a pan, cover well with cold water and bring to the boil. Reduce the heat and simmer for 15 minutes, then drain. Tip into a large bowl and leave to cool completely.

2 Stir the crab, prawns, avocado, pepper, mayonnaise, mirin, sesame seeds and some seasoning into the cooled rice.

3 Put a sheet of seaweed on a large piece of clingfilm. Spread a quarter of the rice mixture along one edge, then roll up as tightly as possible and wrap well in the clingfilm. Repeat the process three times. Chill the rolls in the fridge for 15 minutes to allow the seaweed to soften.

4 To serve, remove the clingfilm and cut each roll in half on a diagonal. Serve with pickled ginger, wasabi paste and soy sauce, if you like, plus a green salad.

Serves 4

Teriyaki Beef Stir-fry

Hands-on time: 20 minutes, plus marinating
Cooking time: 5 minutes

450g (1lb) beef fillet, sliced as thinly as possible, then cut into 1cm (½in) wide strips

2 tbsp vegetable or groundnut oil

225g (8oz) carrots, cut into matchsticks

½ cucumber, seeded and cut into matchsticks

4–6 spring onions, thinly sliced diagonally

noodles tossed in a little sesame oil and wasabi paste (optional) to serve

For the teriyaki marinade

4 tbsp tamari

4 tbsp mirin or medium sherry

1 garlic clove, finely chopped

2.5cm (1in) piece fresh root ginger, peeled and finely chopped

1 First, make the marinade. Put all the ingredients for the marinade in a shallow bowl and mix well. Add the beef and turn to coat. Cover and marinate in the fridge for at least 30 minutes, preferably overnight.

2 Drain the beef, keeping any marinade to one side. Heat a wok or large frying pan, then add the vegetable or groundnut oil and heat until it is smoking. Add the carrots, cucumber and spring onions and fry over a high heat for 2 minutes until the edges are well browned. Remove from the pan and put to one side.

3 Add the beef to the pan and stir-fry over a very high heat for 2 minutes.

4 Put the vegetables back into the pan and add the reserved marinade. Stir-fry for 1–2 minutes until heated through. Serve immediately with noodles tossed in a little sesame oil and a small amount of wasabi paste if you like.

Serves 4

Chicken Chow Mein

Hands-on time: 15 minutes
Cooking time: about 12 minutes

200g (7oz) medium egg noodles

1 tsp sesame oil

400g (14oz) skinless chicken breasts,
    cut into finger-size strips

1½ tsp Chinese five-spice powder

1 tbsp vegetable oil

2 red peppers, seeded and sliced

5 spring onions, thinly sliced

a large handful of bean sprouts

salt and freshly ground black pepper

For the sauce

2.5cm (1in) piece fresh root ginger, peeled
    and grated

2 garlic cloves, crushed

1 tbsp cornflour

1½ tbsp oyster sauce

1½ tbsp tomato ketchup

2 tbsp light soy sauce

1 Start by making the sauce. In a small bowl, mix together the ginger, garlic and cornflour. Whisk in the remaining sauce ingredients and put to one side.

2 Bring a medium pan of water to the boil and cook the noodles according to the pack instructions. Drain well, then toss through the sesame oil to stop them sticking together and put to one side.

3 Put the chicken strips into a large bowl. Toss through the five-spice powder and some seasoning.

4 Heat the vegetable oil in a large wok until smoking. Add the chicken and stir-fry for 5 minutes until golden and cooked through – if you find the chicken is sticking, add a splash of water. Add the peppers, spring onions and bean sprouts and cook for 1–2 minutes until just wilted. Add the noodles and sauce and heat through. Check the seasoning and serve.

Serves 4

Crispy Duck with Mangetouts

Hands-on time: 15 minutes
Cooking time: about 30 minutes, plus cooling

4 duck breast fillets, about 175g (6oz) each

1½ tbsp runny honey

3 tbsp vegetable oil

1 bunch of spring onions, cut into 2.5cm (1in) lengths

1 large green pepper, seeded and cut into thin strips

225g (8oz) mangetouts

2 garlic cloves, crushed

2–3 good pinches of Chinese five-spice powder

3 tbsp caster sugar

3 tbsp dark soy sauce

3 tbsp wine vinegar

16 water chestnuts, sliced

40g (1½oz) toasted cashew nuts

salt

1 Preheat the oven to 180°C (160°C fan oven) mark 4. Prick the duck skin all over with a skewer or fork and rub well with salt. Put the breasts, skin side up, on a rack or trivet in a roasting tin and cook in the oven, uncovered, for 15 minutes.

2 Remove the duck breasts from the oven and brush the skins with honey. Put them back into the oven and cook for a further 5–10 minutes until the duck is cooked through. Leave to cool, then cut into strips.

3 Heat the oil in a wok or large frying pan. Add the spring onions, green pepper, mangetouts, garlic and five-spice powder and stir-fry for 2 minutes. Add the sugar, soy sauce, vinegar and duck strips and toss in the sauce to heat through and glaze. Add the water chestnuts and cook until heated through.

4 Serve immediately, sprinkled with toasted cashew nuts.

Szechuan Beef

Hands-on time: 15 minutes, plus marinating
Cooking time: about 10 minutes

350g (12oz) beef skirt or rump steak, cut into thin strips

5 tbsp hoisin sauce

4 tbsp dry sherry

2 tbsp vegetable oil

2 red or green chillies, finely chopped (see page 80)

1 large onion, thinly sliced

2 garlic cloves, crushed

2 red peppers, seeded and cut into diamond shapes

2.5cm (1in) piece fresh root ginger, peeled and grated

225g can bamboo shoots, drained and sliced

1 tbsp sesame oil

1 Put the beef in a bowl, add the hoisin sauce and sherry and stir to coat. Cover and leave to marinate for 30 minutes.

2 Heat the vegetable oil in a wok or large frying pan until smoking hot. Add the chillies, onion and garlic and stir-fry over a medium heat for 3–4 minutes until softened. Remove with a slotted spoon and put to one side. Add the peppers, increase the heat and stir-fry for a few seconds. Remove and put to one side.

3 Add the steak and marinade to the pan in batches. Stir-fry each batch over a high heat for about 1 minute, removing with a slotted spoon.

4 Put the vegetables back into the pan. Add the ginger and bamboo shoots, then the beef, and stir-fry for a further 1 minute until heated through. Transfer to a warmed serving dish, sprinkle the sesame oil over the top and serve immediately.

Serves 4

Egg Fu Yung

Hands-on time: 10 minutes
Cooking time: about 5 minutes

3 tbsp groundnut or vegetable oil

8 spring onions, finely sliced, plus extra
    spring onion curls to garnish

125g (4oz) shiitake or
    oyster mushrooms, sliced

125g (4oz) canned bamboo shoots,
    drained and chopped

½ green pepper, seeded and
    finely chopped

125g (4oz) frozen peas, thawed

6 medium eggs, beaten

a pinch of salt

2 good pinches of chilli powder

1 tbsp light soy sauce

1 Heat the oil in a wok or large frying pan, add the spring onions, mushrooms, bamboo shoots, pepper and peas and stir-fry for 2–3 minutes.

2 Season the eggs with the salt and chilli powder. Pour the eggs into the pan and continue to cook, stirring, until the egg mixture is set.

3 Sprinkle over the soy sauce and stir well. Serve immediately, garnished with spring onion.

Serves 4

Thai Red Turkey Curry

Hands-on time: 20 minutes
Cooking time: about 25 minutes

3 tbsp vegetable oil

450g (1lb) onions, finely chopped

200g (7oz) green beans, trimmed

125g (4oz) baby sweetcorn, cut on
the diagonal

2 red peppers, seeded and cut into
thick strips

1 tbsp Thai red curry paste, or to taste

1 red chilli, seeded and finely chopped
(see page 80)

1 lemongrass stalk, very finely chopped

4 kaffir lime leaves, bruised

2 tbsp fresh root ginger, peeled and
finely chopped

1 garlic clove, crushed

400ml can coconut milk

600ml (1 pint) chicken or turkey stock

450g (1lb) cooked turkey, cut into strips

150g (5oz) bean sprouts

fresh basil leaves to garnish

1 Heat the oil in a wok or large frying pan, add the onions and cook for 4–5 minutes or until soft.

2 Add the beans, baby corn and peppers to the pan and stir-fry for 3–4 minutes. Add the curry paste, chilli, lemongrass, kaffir lime leaves, ginger and garlic and cook for a further 2 minutes, stirring. Remove from the pan and put to one side.

3 Add the coconut milk and stock to the pan, bring to the boil and bubble vigorously for 5–10 minutes until reduced by one-quarter. Put the vegetables back into the pan with the turkey and bean sprouts. Bring to the boil, reduce the heat and simmer for 1–2 minutes until hot. Serve garnished with basil leaves.

SAVE MONEY

This is a great way to use up
leftover turkey.

Serves 6

Perfect Chilli and Garlic

st of a chilli's heat resides in the seeds and white pith, so it is usually
to remove these, then finely chop or slice the flesh with care. Garlic has
ngent flavour and aroma and can be used raw to flavour dressings and
butters, or fried at the beginning of savoury recipes.

rfect chillies

Cut off the cap and slit open
lengthways. Using a spoon,
scrape out the seeds and the pith
(the hottest parts of the chilli).
For diced chilli, cut into thin
shreds lengthways, then cut
crossways.

Chillies vary enormously in strength,
from quite mild to blisteringly hot,
depending on the type of chilli and
its ripeness. Taste a small piece first
to check it's not too hot for you.

Be extremely careful when
handling chillies not to touch or rub
your eyes with your fingers, as they
will sting. Always wash your hands
thoroughly with soap and water
immediately after handling chillies.
Wash knives immediately after
handling chillies for the same reason.
As a precaution, use rubber gloves
when preparing them, if you like.

1

Perfect garlic

1 Put the clove on the chopping board and put the flat side of a large knife on top of it. Press down firmly on the flat of the blade to crush the clove and break the papery skin.

2 Cut off the base of the clove and slip the garlic out of its skin. It should come away easily.

3 **Slicing** Using a rocking motion with the knife tip on the board, slice the garlic as thinly as you need.

4 **Shredding and chopping** Holding the slices together, shred them across the slices. Chop the shreds if you need chopped garlic.

5 **Crushing** After step 2, the whole clove can be put into a garlic press. To crush with a knife, roughly chop the peeled cloves and put them on the board with a pinch of salt.

6 **Puréeing** Press down hard with the edge of a large knife tip (with the blade facing away from you), then drag the blade along the garlic while still pressing hard. Continue to do this, dragging the knife tip over the garlic.

Chilli Beef Noodle Salad

Hands-on time: 15 minutes, plus soaking

150g (5oz) dried rice noodles

50g (2oz) rocket

125g (4oz) sliced cold roast beef

125g (4oz) sunblush tomatoes, chopped

For the Thai dressing

juice of 1 lime

1 lemongrass stalk, outside leaves
   discarded, trimmed and
   finely chopped

1 red chilli, seeded and chopped
   (see page 80)

2 tsp finely chopped fresh root ginger

2 garlic cloves, crushed

1 tbsp Thai fish sauce

3 tbsp extra virgin olive oil

salt and freshly ground black pepper

1 Put the noodles into a large bowl and
   pour boiling water over them to cover.
   Put to one side for 15 minutes.

2 To make the dressing, whisk together
   the lime juice, lemongrass, chilli,
   ginger, garlic, fish sauce and oil in
   a small bowl and season with salt
   and ground black pepper.

3 While they are still warm, drain the
   noodles well, put into a large bowl and
   toss with the dressing. Leave to cool.

4 Just before serving, toss the rocket,
   sliced beef and tomatoes through
   the noodles.

Serves 4

Thai Green Curry

Hands-on time: 15 minutes
Cooking time: about 15 minutes

2 tsp vegetable oil

1 green chilli, seeded and finely chopped (see page 80)

4cm (1½in) piece fresh root ginger, peeled and finely grated

1 lemongrass stalk, trimmed and cut into three pieces

225g (8oz) brown-cap or oyster mushrooms

1 tbsp Thai green curry paste

300ml (½ pint) coconut milk

150ml (¼ pint) chicken stock

1 tbsp Thai fish sauce

1 tsp light soy sauce

350g (12oz) boneless, skinless chicken breasts, cut into bite-size pieces

350g (12oz) cooked peeled king prawns

fresh coriander sprigs to garnish

Thai fragrant rice to serve

1 Heat the oil in a wok or large frying pan, add the chilli, ginger, lemongrass and mushrooms and stir-fry for about 3 minutes until the mushrooms begin to turn golden. Add the curry paste and fry for a further 1 minute.

2 Pour in the coconut milk, stock, fish sauce and soy sauce and bring to the boil. Stir in the chicken, then reduce the heat and simmer for about 8 minutes until the chicken is cooked.

3 Add the prawns and cook for a further 1 minute. Garnish with coriander sprigs and serve immediately, with Thai fragrant rice.

Quick Pad Thai

Hands-on time: 12 minutes, plus soaking
Cooking time: 8 minutes

250g (9oz) wide ribbon rice noodles

3 tbsp satay and sweet chilli pesto

125g (4oz) mangetouts, thinly sliced

125g (4oz) sugarsnap peas, thinly sliced

3 medium eggs, beaten

3 tbsp chilli soy sauce, plus extra
   to serve

250g (9oz) cooked peeled tiger prawns

25g (1oz) dry-roasted peanuts,
   roughly crushed

lime wedges to serve (optional)

1 Put the noodles in a heatproof bowl, cover with boiling water and soak for 4 minutes until softened. Drain, rinse under cold water and put to one side.

2 Heat a wok or large frying pan until hot, add the chilli pesto and stir-fry for 1 minute. Add the mangetouts and sugarsnap peas and cook for a further 2 minutes. Tip into a bowl. Put the pan back on the heat, add the eggs and cook, stirring, for 1 minute.

3 Add the soy sauce, prawns and noodles to the pan. Toss well and cook for 3 minutes until piping hot. Put the vegetables back into the pan and cook for a further 1 minute until heated through, then sprinkle with the peanuts. Serve with extra soy sauce and lime wedges to squeeze over, if you like.

Thai Vegetable Curry

Hands-on time: 10 minutes
Cooking time: 15 minutes

2–3 tbsp red Thai curry paste

2.5cm (1in) piece fresh root ginger,
   peeled and finely chopped

50g (2oz) cashew nuts

400ml can coconut milk

3 carrots, cut into thin batons

1 broccoli head, cut into florets

20g (¾oz) fresh coriander,
   roughly chopped

zest and juice of 1 lime

2 large handfuls of spinach leaves

boiled basmati rice to serve

1 Put the curry paste into a large pan,
   add the ginger and nuts and stir-fry
   over a medium heat for 2–3 minutes.

2 Add the coconut milk, cover and bring
   to the boil. Stir the carrots into the
   pan, then reduce the heat and simmer
   for 5 minutes. Add the broccoli florets
   and simmer for a further 5 minutes or
   until tender.

3 Stir the coriander and lime zest into
   the pan with the spinach. Squeeze the
   lime juice over and serve with rice.

Serves 4

Thai Noodle Salad

Hands-on time: 20 minutes, plus soaking
Cooking time: about 8 minutes

200g (7oz) sugarsnap peas, trimmed

250g pack of Thai stir-fry rice noodles

100g (3½oz) cashew nuts

300g (11oz) carrots, cut into batons

10 spring onions, sliced on the diagonal

300g (11oz) bean sprouts

20g (¾oz) fresh coriander, roughly chopped, plus fresh coriander sprigs to garnish

1 red bird's eye chilli, seeded and finely chopped (see page 80)

2 tsp sweet chilli sauce

4 tbsp sesame oil

6 tbsp soy sauce

juice of 2 limes

salt and freshly ground black pepper

1 Bring a pan of salted water to the boil and blanch the sugarsnap peas for 2–3 minutes until just tender to the bite. Drain and refresh under cold water.

2 Put the noodles into a bowl, cover with boiling water and leave to soak for 4 minutes. Rinse under cold water and drain very well.

3 Toast the cashews in a dry frying pan until golden – about 5 minutes.

4 Put the sugarsnaps into a large glass serving bowl. Add the carrots, spring onions, bean sprouts, chopped coriander, chopped chilli, cashews and noodles.

5 Mix the chilli sauce with the oil, soy sauce and lime juice and season well with salt and ground black pepper. Pour over the salad and toss together, then garnish with coriander sprigs and serve.

Serves 4

American Classics

Buttermilk Fried Chicken and Barbecue Beans

🍴 **Hands-on time:** 25 minutes, plus chilling
Cooking time: about 20 minutes

8 chicken drumsticks, about 800g (1¾lb)
284ml pot buttermilk
sunflower oil to deep-fry
150g (5oz) plain flour
2 tsp cayenne pepper
1 tsp garlic granules
1 tsp dried thyme
salt and freshly ground black pepper

For the beans

2 × 400g cans baked beans
1 tbsp barbecue sauce
1 tbsp soy sauce

1 Put the chicken pieces into a large bowl. Stir through the buttermilk and season with salt and ground black pepper. Cover and chill for 5 hours.

2 When ready, half-fill a deep-fat fryer with sunflower oil and heat to 160°C (test by frying a small cube of bread; it should brown in 60 seconds). Stir together the flour, cayenne pepper, garlic granules, thyme and some seasoning and tip on to a plate. Keeping as much buttermilk on the chicken as possible, start by dipping half the drumsticks into the flour to coat completely.

3 Carefully lower the chicken drumsticks into the hot oil and deep-fry for 10 minutes until deep golden, crispy and cooked through. Drain on kitchen paper, season with salt and loosely cover with foil to keep warm. Repeat coating and cooking with the remaining chicken.

4 While the final batch of chicken is cooking, heat the baked beans in a pan with the barbecue and soy sauces until piping hot. Serve the chicken with the beans.

SAVE TIME

To get ahead, fry the drumsticks up to 5 hours in advance. Cool, then cover and chill. Reheat in a preheated oven at 200°C (180°C fan oven) mark 6 for 15–20 minutes until hot.

Serves 4

Buffalo Wings and Ranch Dressing Dip

Hands-on time: 20 minutes
Cooking time: about 55 minutes

1.1kg (2½lb) chicken wings

1 tsp sunflower oil

100g (3½oz) tomato ketchup

½ tbsp hot chilli sauce

15g (½oz) butter

2 tsp white wine vinegar

2 tsp cornflour

For the dip

100ml (3½fl oz) soured cream

1 tbsp mayonnaise

½ tsp garlic granules

1 tbsp freshly chopped chives

1 Preheat the oven to 220°C (200°C fan oven) mark 7. Put the chicken wings into a roasting tin, drizzle over the oil and season well. Cook for 35–40 minutes until golden.

2 In a small pan, heat the tomato ketchup, chilli sauce, butter and vinegar until melted and smooth. Take off the heat, stir in the cornflour, then pour the mixture over the chicken and toss to coat. Put the chicken back into the oven to cook for a further 10–15 minutes until the sauce is sticky.

3 To make the dip, stir all the ingredients together in a small bowl, then season to taste. Serve the wings with the dip.

Makes about 12 wings

Sticky Ribs with Rice and Beans

Hands-on time: 15 minutes
Cooking time: about 55 minutes

125g (4oz) tomato ketchup

1½ tbsp soy sauce

1½ tbsp white wine vinegar

3 tbsp honey

1½ tsp mixed spice

½ tsp hot chilli powder

1.5kg (3¼lb) individual pork spare ribs

250g (9oz) basmati rice

400g can kidney beans, drained and rinsed

a large handful of fresh coriander, chopped

green salad to serve

1 Preheat the oven to 200°C (180°C fan oven) mark 6. Line a large roasting tin with a double layer of foil. In a large bowl, mix together the first six ingredients. Add the ribs to the bowl and stir to coat completely, then empty the ribs and glaze into the lined roasting tin and spread out evenly.

2 Cover with foil and cook in the oven for 20 minutes. Uncover, then turn the ribs and put back into the oven for 30–35 minutes, turning in the glaze occasionally, until they're dark and sticky (most of the liquid should have evaporated).

3 Meanwhile, cook the rice according to the pack instructions, adding the kidney beans for the final 2 minutes of cooking. Drain well and stir in the coriander. Serve the rice with the ribs and a green salad.

Serves 4

American-style Hamburgers

Hands-on time: 20 minutes, plus chilling
Cooking time: 10 minutes

1kg (2¼lb) extra-lean minced beef

2 tsp salt

2 tbsp steak seasoning

sunflower oil to greas and brush

6 large soft rolls, halved

6 thin-cut slices havarti or raclette cheese

4 small cocktail gherkins, sliced
  lengthways

6 tbsp mustard mayonnaise

6 lettuce leaves, such as frisée

4 large vine-ripened tomatoes,
  sliced thickly

2 large shallots, sliced into thin rings

freshly ground black pepper

1 Put the minced beef into a large bowl and add the salt, steak seasoning and plenty of ground black pepper. Use your hands to mix all the ingredients together thoroughly. Lightly oil the inside of six 10cm (4in) rösti rings and put on a foil-lined baking sheet. Press the meat firmly into the rings, or use your hands to shape the mixture into six even-sized patties. Cover with clingfilm and chill for at least 1 hour.

2 Heat a large griddle pan until it's really hot. Put the rolls, cut sides down, on the griddle and toast.

3 Lightly oil the griddle, ease the burgers out of the moulds and brush with oil. Cook over a medium heat for about 3 minutes, then turn the burgers over carefully. Put a slice of cheese and a few slices of gherkin on top of each and cook for a further 3 minutes. While the burgers are cooking, spread the mustard mayonnaise on the toasted side of the rolls. Add the lettuce, tomatoes and shallots. Put the burgers on top and sandwich with the other half-rolls.

Serves 6

Cajun Fish Wraps

Hands-on time: 15 minutes
Cooking time: about 5 minutes

zest and juice of ½ lime

4 tbsp natural yogurt

1 tbsp freshly chopped chives

25g (1oz) dry polenta

1 tbsp cajun spice

375g (13oz) white fish fillets, such as plaice, cod or pollock, cut into finger-size strips

oil to brush

50g (2oz) rocket leaves

1 avocado, cut into strips

1 red pepper, seeded and cut into strips

4 flour tortillas

salt and freshly ground black pepper

green salad to serve

1 In a bowl, mix together the lime zest and juice, yogurt, chives and some seasoning. Put to one side.

2 Preheat the grill to high. In a medium bowl, mix together the polenta, cajun spice and a little seasoning. Add the fish and coat in the polenta mixture. Brush a baking tray with some oil and arrange the coated fish on the tray. Grill the fish for 3–5 minutes until cooked through.

3 Divide the fish, rocket, avocado and pepper equally into four, putting the ingredients in one quarter of each tortilla. Drizzle over the yogurt dressing, then fold each tortilla into quarters to make a pocket. Serve immediately with a green salad.

Serves 4

Tex-Mex Veggie Burgers

Hands-on time: 20 minutes
Cooking time: 10 minutes

410g can black-eyed beans, drained
 and rinsed

410g can kidney beans, drained
 and rinsed

150g (5oz) sweetcorn

2 tbsp sliced jalapeño peppers

a small handful of fresh coriander,
 plus extra to garnish

2 medium eggs

75g (3oz) fresh or dried white
 breadcrumbs

1 tbsp olive oil

To serve

4 burger buns, toasted (optional)

1 avocado, peeled, stoned and
 thinly sliced

4 tsp soured cream

4 tsp tomato salsa

1 Put the first five ingredients and plenty of seasoning into a food processor and pulse briefly until combined but still with chunky texture. Empty into a large bowl and stir through the eggs and breadcrumbs. Form into four patties.

2 Heat the oil in a large non-stick frying pan and gently fry the patties for 8–10 minutes, carefully turning once, until golden and piping hot.

3 Serve the burgers on toasted buns, if you like, topped with avocado slices, a small dollop of soured cream and some tomato salsa.

Serves 4

Lentil Chilli

Hands-on time: 15 minutes
Cooking time: about 25 minutes

1 tbsp vegetable oil

1 red onion, finely chopped

1 tsp each ground cumin, coriander
and chilli powder

2 × 400g cans chopped tomatoes

1 vegetable stock cube, crumbled

2 × 400g cans lentils, drained and rinsed

400g can kidney beans, drained
and rinsed

a handful of fresh coriander, chopped

crisp flatbreads or boiled brown rice
to serve

1 Heat the oil in a large pan, add the
onion and fry for 10 minutes until soft.
Add the ground spices and cook for a
further minute. Stir in the tomatoes,
stock cube and lentils and simmer
for 10 minutes until thickened.

2 Add the kidney beans and heat
through. Stir through most of the
coriander and check the seasoning.
Garnish with the remaining coriander
and serve with crisp flatbreads or
brown rice.

Macaroni Cheese

Hands-on time: 15 minutes
Cooking time: about 15 minutes

450g (1lb) macaroni pasta
40g (1½oz) each butter and plain flour
500ml (17fl oz) semi-skimmed milk
125g (4oz) mature Cheddar, grated
25g (1oz) fresh white breadcrumbs
salt and freshly ground black pepper
green salad to serve

1 Bring a large pan of salted water to the boil and cook the macaroni pasta for 5-8 minutes until just tender. Drain.

2 Meanwhile, melt the butter in a large pan. Stir in the flour and cook for 1 minute. Take off the heat and gradually beat in the milk using a wooden spoon. Heat gently, stirring constantly, until the mixture thickens, about 3-5 minutes. Take off the heat, stir in 75g (3oz) of the cheese and the drained macaroni. Check the seasoning.

3 Preheat the grill to medium. Empty the macaroni mixture into a 2 litre (3½ pint) ovenproof serving dish. Top with the remaining cheese and breadcrumbs. Grill for about 5 minutes until piping hot and golden. Serve immediately with a green salad.

Serves 4

Sides

Tzatziki

To serve eight, you will need:
1 cucumber, 300g (11oz) Greek-style
yogurt, 2 tsp olive oil, 2 tbsp freshly
chopped mint, 1 large garlic clove,
crushed, salt and freshly ground
black pepper, warm pitta bread and
vegetable sticks to serve.

1   Halve, seed and dice the
    cucumber and put into a bowl.
2   Add the yogurt and oil. Stir in
    the chopped mint and garlic,
    and season with salt and ground
    black pepper to taste. Cover and
    chill in the fridge until ready
    to serve.
3   Serve with warm pitta bread and
    vegetable sticks.

Taramasalata

To serve six, you will need:
100g (3½oz) country-style bread,
crusts removed, 75g (3oz) smoked
cod roe, 2 tbsp lemon juice, 100ml
(3½fl oz) light olive oil, freshly
ground black pepper, warm pitta
bread or toasted flatbreads to serve.

1   Put the bread into a bowl, cover
    with cold water and leave to soak
    for 10 minutes. Drain and squeeze
    out most of the water.
2   Soak the smoked cod roe in cold
    water to cover for 10 minutes, then
    drain and remove the skin.
3   Put the roe in a blender or food
    processor with the bread and whiz
    for 30 seconds. With the motor
    running, add the lemon juice and
    oil, and whiz briefly to combine.
    Season with ground black pepper
    to taste.
4   Spoon into a bowl, cover and chill
    until needed. Serve with warm
    pitta bread or toasted flatbreads.

Blue Cheese Dip

To serve six, you will need:
150ml (¼ pint) soured cream, 1 garlic
clove, crushed, 175g (6oz) blue Stilton,
juice of 1 lemon, salt and freshly
ground black pepper, snipped chives
to garnish, vegetable sticks to serve.

1 Put all the ingredients into a
   blender or food processor and
   work to a smooth paste.
2 Transfer to a serving dish and
   chill until required. Check the
   seasoning, sprinkle with chives
   and serve with a selection of
   vegetable sticks.

Red Pepper and Feta Dip

To make about 25 tbsp (375g/13oz),
you will need: 290g jar roasted red
peppers, drained, 200g (7oz) feta,
crumbled, 1 small garlic clove, 1 tbsp
natural yogurt and toasted pitta
bread to serve.

1 Put all the ingredients into a
   blender or food processor and
   whiz until smooth. Serve the dip
   with strips of toasted pitta bread.

Guacamole

To serve six, you will need: 2 ripe
avocados, 2 small tomatoes, seeded
and chopped, juice of 2 limes, 2 tbsp
extra virgin olive oil, 2 tbsp freshly
chopped coriander, salt and freshly
ground black pepper, tortilla chips
or warm pitta bread and vegetable
sticks to serve.

1 Cut the avocados in half, remove
   the stones and peel away the skin.
   Tip the flesh into a bowl and mash
   with a fork.
2 Quickly add the tomatoes, lime
   juice, oil and chopped coriander.
   Mix well and season with salt
   and ground black pepper to taste.
   Cover and chill until ready to serve.
3 Serve the guacamole with tortilla
   chips or warm pitta bread and
   vegetable sticks.

Tortilla Chips for Dips

8 flour tortillas
2 tbsp olive oil
¼–½ tsp smoked paprika
salt
dips to serve

1 Preheat the oven to 200°C (180°C fan oven) mark 6. Stack the flour tortillas on top of each other, then cut through the stack like a pizza to make eight wedges. Put the triangles into a large bowl with the oil, smoked paprika and lots of salt.

2 Use your hands to mix everything together, making sure all the triangles are covered with the oil and spice. Divide the triangles between two baking sheets.

3 Cook for 12–20 minutes, tossing occasionally, until golden and crisp. Leave to cool completely before serving with your favourite dips.

SAVE TIME

To get ahead, make up to two days in advance. Keep in an airtight tin.

Serves 10

Classic Houmous

 Hands-on time: 5 minutes

400g can chickpeas

40ml (1½fl oz) olive oil, plus extra
  to drizzle

1½ tbsp lemon juice

1 small garlic clove

¼ tsp ground cumin

salt and freshly ground black pepper

sprinkle of paprika or cayenne pepper
  (optional)

breadsticks and toasted pitta bread
  to serve

1. Drain and rinse the chickpeas. Put a spoonful to one side then put the rest into a food processor with the oil, lemon juice, 1 tbsp water, garlic, ground cumin and plenty of seasoning. Whiz until smooth, then check the seasoning.

2. Scrape into a serving dish. Garnish with the reserved chickpeas, a sprinkle of paprika or cayenne pepper, if you like, and a drizzle of oil. Serve with breadsticks and toasted pitta bread for scooping.

Serves 6

Pitta Bread

Hands-on time 20 minutes, plus rising
Cooking time: about 8 minutes per batch, plus cooling

15g (½oz) fresh yeast or
    1½ tsp traditional dried yeast and
    1 tsp sugar

700g (1½lb) strong white flour, plus extra
    to dust

1 tsp salt

1 tbsp caster sugar

1 tbsp olive oil, plus extra to grease

1 Blend the fresh yeast with 450ml
(¾ pint) tepid water. If using dried
yeast, sprinkle it into the water with
the sugar and leave in a warm place
for 15 minutes or until frothy.

2 Put the flour, salt and sugar into a
bowl, make a well in the centre and
pour in the yeast liquid with the oil.
Mix to a smooth dough, then turn out
on to a lightly floured worksurface and
knead for 10 minutes or until smooth
and elastic.

3 Place the dough in a large bowl, cover
with oiled clingfilm and leave to rise in
a warm place until doubled in size.

4 Divide the dough into 16 pieces and roll
each into an oval shape about 20.5cm
(8in) long. Place on floured baking
sheets, cover with oiled clingfilm
and leave in a warm place for about
30 minutes until slightly risen and puffy.
Preheat the oven to 240°C (220°C fan
oven) mark 9.

5 Bake the pittas in batches for 5–8
minutes only. They should be just lightly
browned on top. Remove from the oven
and wrap in a clean tea towel. Repeat
with the remaining pittas.

6 When the pittas are warm enough
to handle, but not completely cold,
transfer them to a plastic bag and
leave until cold. This will ensure that
they have a soft crust.

7 To serve, warm in the oven, or toast
lightly. Split and fill with salad, cheese,
cold meats or your favourite sandwich
filling. Or, cut into strips and serve
with dips.

Makes 16 pitta breads

Balsamic Dressing

To make about 100ml (3½fl oz), you will need: 2 tbsp balsamic vinegar, 4 tbsp extra virgin olive oil, salt and freshly ground black pepper.

1 Whisk the vinegar and oil in a small bowl. Season with salt and ground black pepper to taste.
2 If not using immediately, store in a cool place and whisk briefly before using.

Basic Vinaigrette

To make about 300ml (½ pint), you will need: 100ml (3½fl oz) extra virgin olive oil, 100ml (3½fl oz) grapeseed oil, 50ml (2fl oz) white wine vinegar, a pinch each of sugar and English mustard powder, 1 garlic clove, crushed (optional), salt and freshly ground black pepper.

1 Put both oils, the vinegar, sugar, mustard powder and garlic, if you like, into a large screw-topped jar. Tighten the lid and shake well. Season to taste with salt and ground black pepper.
2 If not using immediately, store in a cool place and shake briefly before using.

To help it emulsify easily, add 1 tsp cold water to the dressing. To get a really good emulsion, shake the dressing vigorously in a screw-topped jar.

French Dressing

To make 100ml (3½fl oz), you will need: 1 tsp Dijon mustard, a pinch of sugar, 1 tbsp red or white wine vinegar, 6 tbsp extra virgin olive oil, salt and freshly ground black pepper.

1 Put the mustard, sugar and vinegar into a small bowl and season with salt and ground black pepper. Whisk thoroughly until well combined, then gradually whisk in the oil until thoroughly combined.
2 If not using immediately, store in a cool place and whisk briefly before using.

Variations
Herb Dressing
Use half the mustard, replace the vinegar with lemon juice, and add 2 tbsp freshly chopped herbs, such as parsley, chervil and chives.
Garlic Dressing
Add 1 crushed garlic clove to the dressing in step 2.

Caesar Dressing

To make about 150ml (¼ pint), you will need: 1 medium egg, 1 garlic clove, juice of ½ lemon, 2 tsp Dijon mustard, 1 tsp balsamic vinegar, 150ml (¼ pint) sunflower oil, salt and freshly ground black pepper.

1 Put the egg, garlic, lemon juice, mustard and vinegar into a food processor and whiz until smooth, then, with the motor running, gradually add the oil and whiz until smooth. Season with salt and ground black pepper.
2 If not using immediately, cover and chill for up to three days. Whisk briefly before using.

Note: As this dressing contains raw eggs, buy those with the British Lion mark and don't serve to vulnerable groups.

Mixed Green Salad

Hands-on time: 10 minutes

3 round lettuce hearts, roughly shredded

100g (3½oz) watercress

2 ripe avocados, roughly chopped

1 box salad cress, chopped

100g (3½oz) sugarsnap peas,
roughly sliced

For the vinaigrette dressing

1 tbsp white wine vinegar

4 tbsp olive oil

salt and freshly ground black pepper

1 Put the lettuce hearts into a bowl and add the watercress, avocados, salad cress and sugarsnap peas.

2 To make the vinaigrette dressing, put all the ingredients into a screw-topped jar, secure the lid tightly and shake vigorously to mix. Pour the dressing over the salad and toss to mix. Serve immediately.

Serves 8

Classic Coleslaw

¼ each medium red and white cabbage, shredded

1 carrot, grated

20g (¾oz) fresh flat-leafed parsley, finely chopped

For the dressing

1½ tbsp red wine vinegar

4 tbsp olive oil

½ tsp Dijon mustard

salt and freshly ground black pepper

1 To make the dressing, put the vinegar into a small bowl, add the oil and mustard, season well with salt and ground black pepper and mix well.

2 Put the cabbage and carrot into a large bowl and toss to mix well. Add the parsley.

3 Mix the dressing again, pour over the cabbage mixture and toss well to coat.

Serves 6

Crunchy Ribbon Salad

Hands-on time: 10 minutes

2 large carrots, trimmed

1 cucumber

1 courgette

2 tbsp sweet chilli sauce

1 tbsp white wine vinegar

salt and freshly ground black pepper

1 Use a vegetable peeler to make carrot ribbons. Put the ribbons into a large bowl. Trim the cucumber and courgette and peel both into ribbons. Add to the carrots.

2 Pour the sweet chilli sauce and vinegar over the vegetables and season with salt and ground black pepper. Use your hands to toss everything together. Serve immediately.

SAVE TIME

To get ahead, complete step 1 up to 2 hours in advance. Cover with damp kitchen paper, then chill. Bring to room temperature, then complete step 2 to serve.

Serves 6

Corn-on-the-cob with Chilli Lime Butter

Hands-on time: 15 minutes, plus chilling
Cooking time: about 8 minutes

4 corn-on-the-cobs

For the chilli lime butter

125g (4oz) unsalted butter, slightly softened

1 tbsp sweet chilli sauce

2 tbsp lime juice

salt and freshly ground black pepper

1 First prepare the chilli lime butter. In a bowl, mix the butter with the chilli sauce and lime juice, then season with salt and ground black pepper. Put on a piece of clingfilm, roll into a log, wrap well and chill to firm up.

2 Strip the outer husks from the corn cobs and trim the bases. Bring a large pan of water to the boil, add the corn cobs and cook for 6–8 minutes until tender. (Don't add salt to the cooking water, or it will toughen the corn.)

3 Drain the corn cobs and serve, topped with slices of chilli lime butter.

Serves 4

Griddled Garlic Bread

Hands-on time: 5 minutes
Cooking time: about 6 minutes

1 large crusty loaf

175g (6oz) butter, cubed

3 garlic cloves, peeled and crushed

salt and freshly ground black pepper

1 Preheat the grill. Cut the bread into thick slices.

2 Put the butter and garlic into a small pan and heat gently until melted. Season with salt and ground black pepper.

3 Spoon some of the melted butter on to one side of each slice of bread. Put the slices, buttered-side down, on the grill rack. Cook for 1–2 minutes until crisp and golden. Drizzle the uppermost sides with the remaining butter, turn over and cook the other side. Serve immediately.

Serves 8

Garlic and Coriander Naans

Hands-on time: 10 minutes
Cooking time: about 10 minutes

225g (8oz) strong white flour,
   plus extra to dust

1 tbsp caster sugar

2½ tsp baking powder

2 tsp black onion seeds

1 tbsp freeze-dried coriander

¾ tsp salt

150ml (¼ pint) milk

2 garlic cloves, crushed

1 tbsp vegetable oil

1 Put the flour, sugar, baking powder, onion seeds, coriander and salt into a large bowl. Stir. Heat the milk and garlic until just warm, then pour into the bowl and mix to a dough. Knead well to bring together.

2 Divide the dough into four and roll each portion out on a lightly floured worksurface to an oval measuring about 9cm x 17cm (3½in x 6½in).

3 Heat the oil in a large pan over a medium heat and fry the naans for 5 minutes, turning once, or until spotted golden on both sides (you can do this in batches if necessary). Serve immediately.

SAVE TIME

To get ahead, make naan breads up to 5 hours in advance. Reheat in a toaster and serve immediately.

Perfect Deep-frying

Carrots, broccoli, onions, courgettes, aubergines, mushrooms, peppers and cauliflower are all good deep-fried in a light batter.

Deep-fried Mixed Vegetables

To serve four, you will need: About 900g (2lb) mixed vegetables (such as aubergines, broccoli, cauliflower, red peppers), cut into small, similar-size pieces, vegetable oil to deep-fry, 125g (4oz) plain flour, plus extra to coat, 125g (4oz) cornflour, a pinch of salt, 1 medium egg yolk, 300ml (½ pint) sparkling water.

1. Prepare the vegetables and cut into small pieces (no more than 2cm (¾in) thick). Dry well on kitchen paper.
2. Heat the oil in a deep-fryer to 170°C (a small cube of bread should brown in 40 seconds).
3. To make the batter, lightly whisk together the flour, cornflour, salt, egg yolk and water.
4. Coat the vegetables lightly with flour, then dip into the batter.
5. Fry in batches, a few pieces at a time, until the batter is crisp and golden brown. Don't put too many vegetables in the pan at once (if you do, the temperature drops and the vegetables take longer to cook and become greasy). Remove with a slotted spoon and drain on kitchen paper before serving.

5

Onion Bhajis

Hands-on time: 20 minutes
Cooking time: 15 minutes

450g (1lb) onions, halved and
thinly sliced

1 garlic clove, finely chopped

2.5cm (1in) piece fresh root ginger,
peeled and finely chopped

1–2 hot red chillies, peeled, seeded,
if you like, and chopped (see page 80)

1 tsp ground turmeric

1 tsp ground cardamom seeds

125g (4oz) gram or plain wholemeal
flour, sifted

50g (2oz) self-raising flour

3 tbsp freshly chopped mint

1 tbsp lemon juice

oil to deep-fry

salt and freshly ground black pepper

mint sprigs and lime wedges, to garnish

1 Put the onions, garlic, ginger and
chillies into a bowl. Add the ground
spices and toss well. Add the flours,
mint and salt and ground black
pepper. Mix thoroughly. Add the
lemon juice and about 5 tbsp cold
water or enough to make the mixture
cling together; do not make it too wet.

2 Heat the oil in a deep-fat fryer. Test by
frying a small cube of bread; it should
sizzle immediately and rise to the
surface. Remove with a slotted spoon.

3 Divide the mixture into 12 portions.
Using dampened hands, shape each
into a ball. Pat firmly to ensure that it
will hold together during cooking.

4 Deep-fry three to four bhajis at a time
for 5 minutes or until golden brown
on all sides. Carefully remove from
the hot oil and drain on crumpled
kitchen paper. Serve the bhajis warm,
garnished with mint sprigs and
lime wedges.

SAVE TIME

To get ahead, deep-fry and drain
the bhajis as in step 4. To use,
reheat on a baking sheet at 200°C
(180°C fan oven) mark 6 for about
10 minutes before serving.

Makes 12

Vegetable Tempura

Hands-on time: 20 minutes
Cooking time: 15 minutes

125g (4oz) plain flour, plus 2 tbsp extra
  to sprinkle

2 tbsp cornflour

2 tbsp arrowroot

125g (4oz) cauliflower, cut into
  small florets

2 large carrots, cut into matchsticks

16 button mushrooms

2 courgettes, sliced

2 red peppers, seeded and sliced

vegetable oil to deep-fry

salt and freshly ground black pepper

fresh coriander sprigs to garnish

For the dipping sauce

25g (1oz) piece fresh root ginger, peeled
  and grated

4 tbsp dry sherry

2 tbsp soy sauce

1 Sift 125g (4oz) flour, the cornflour and arrowroot into a large bowl with a pinch each of salt and ground black pepper. Gradually whisk in 300ml (½ pint) ice-cold water to form a thin batter. Cover and chill.

2 To make the dipping sauce, put the ginger, sherry and soy sauce in a heatproof bowl and pour over 200ml (7fl oz) boiling water. Stir well to mix, then put to one side.

3 Put the vegetables in a large bowl and sprinkle over 2 tbsp flour. Toss well to coat. Heat the oil in a wok or deep-fryer to 170°C (test by frying a small cube of bread; it should brown in 40 seconds).

4 Dip a handful of the vegetables in the batter, then remove with a slotted spoon, taking up a lot of the batter with the vegetables. Add to the hot oil and deep-fry for 3–5 minutes until crisp and golden. Remove with a slotted spoon and drain on kitchen paper; keep them hot while you cook the remaining batches. Serve immediately, garnished with coriander sprigs and accompanied by the dipping sauce.

138

Serves 4

Two-tone Chips

Hands-on time: 10 minutes
Cooking time: about 45 minutes

3 large sweet potatoes, about
  700g (1½lb)
3 large baking potatoes, about
  900g (2lb)
4 tbsp olive oil
few pinches of dried chilli flakes
salt and freshly ground black pepper

1 Preheat the oven to 200°C (180°C fan oven) mark 6. Cut both types of potatoes into wedges and put into a bowl. Pour over the oil, then sprinkle over the chilli flakes and season with salt and ground black pepper.

2 Spread out over two non-stick baking trays and cook for 40–45 minutes, turning occasionally, until tender and golden. Serve immediately.

SAVE TIME

To get ahead, prepare to the end of step 1 up to 1 hour before. Cover and put to one side. Complete the recipe to serve.

Serves 8

Perfect Rice

Rice is an incredibly versatile grain. Like pasta, it is the perfect storecupboard standby. Stored in an airtight container in a cool, dry place, it has a shelf life of at least a year.

Cooking rice

There are two main types of rice: long-grain and short-grain. Long-grain rice is generally served as an accompaniment; the most commonly used type of long-grain rice in South-east Asian cooking is jasmine rice, also known as Thai fragrant rice. It has a distinctive taste and slightly sticky texture. Long-grain rice needs no special preparation, although it should be washed to remove excess starch. Put the rice in a bowl and cover with cold water. Stir until this becomes cloudy, then drain and repeat until the water is clear.

Long-grain rice

1. Use 50–75g (2–3oz) raw rice per person; measured by volume 50–75ml (2–2½fl oz). Measure the rice by volume and put it in a pan with a pinch of salt and twice the volume of boiling water (or stock).
2. Bring to the boil. Reduce the heat to low and set the timer for the time stated on the pack. The rice should be al dente: tender with a bite at the centre.
3. When the rice is cooked, fluff up the grains with a fork.

Basmati rice

Put the rice in a bowl and cover with cold water. Stir until this becomes cloudy, then drain and repeat until the water is clear. Soak the rice for 30 minutes, then drain before cooking.

Perfect rice

- ❑ Use 50–75g (2–3oz) raw rice per person – or measure by volume 50–75ml (2–2½fl oz)
- ❑ If you cook rice often, you may want to invest in a special rice steamer. They are available in Asian supermarkets and some kitchen shops and give good, consistent results

Basic Pilau Rice

Hands-on time: 5 minutes
Cooking time: 20 minutes, plus standing

50g (2oz) butter
225g (8oz) long-grain white rice
750ml (1¼ pints) chicken stock
salt and freshly ground black pepper
generous knob of butter to serve

1 Melt the butter in a pan, add the rice and fry gently for 3–4 minutes until translucent.

2 Slowly pour in the stock, season, stir and cover with a tight-fitting lid. Leave, undisturbed, over a very low heat for about 15 minutes or until the water has been absorbed and the rice is just tender.

3 Remove the lid and cover the surface of the rice with a clean cloth. Replace the lid and leave to stand in a warm place for about 15 minutes to dry the rice before serving.

4 Fork through and add a knob of butter to serve.

Serves 4

Simple Fried Rice

Hands-on time: 5 minutes
Cooking time: about 20 minutes

150g (5oz) long-grain rice

2 tbsp sesame oil

3 medium eggs, lightly beaten

250g (9oz) frozen petits pois

250g (9oz) cooked peeled prawns

1 Cook the rice in boiling water for about 10 minutes or according to the pack instructions. Drain well.

2 Heat 1 tsp sesame oil in a large non-stick frying pan. Pour in half the beaten eggs and tilt the pan around over the heat for about 1 minute until the egg is set. Tip the omelette on to a warmed plate. Repeat with another 1 tsp sesame oil and the remaining beaten egg to make another omelette. Tip on to another warmed plate.

3 Add the remaining oil to the pan and stir in the rice and peas. Stir-fry for 2–3 minutes until the peas are cooked. Stir in the prawns.

4 Roll up the omelettes, roughly chop one-third of one, then slice the remainder into strips. Add the chopped omelette to the rice, peas and prawns, and cook for 1–2 minutes until heated through. Divide the fried rice among four serving bowls, top with the sliced omelette and serve immediately.

Serves 4

Perfect Noodles

Noodles, along with rice, are one of the staples of Asian cooking. Often served as an accompaniment to stir-fried dishes, they can also be cooked and added as one of the ingredients.

Egg (wheat) noodles

These are the most versatile of Asian noodles. Like Italian pasta, they are made from wheat flour, egg and water and are available fresh or dried in various thicknesses.

Cooking noodles

1. Bring a pan of water to the boil and put the noodles in.
2. Agitate the noodles using chopsticks or a fork to separate them. This can take a minute or even more.
3. Continue boiling for 4–5 minutes until the noodles are cooked al dente: tender but with a little bite in the centre.
4. Drain well and then rinse in cold water and toss with a little oil if you are not planning to use them immediately.

Glass, cellophane or bean thread noodles

These very thin noodles are made from mung beans; they need only 1 minute in boiling water.

Rice noodles

These may be very fine (rice vermicelli) or thick and flat. Most need no cooking, only soaking in warm or hot water; check the pack instructions, or cover the noodles with freshly boiled water and soak until they are al dente: tender but with a little bite in the centre. Drain well and toss with a little oil if you are not using them immediately.

Perfect noodles

- ❑ Use 50–75g (2–3oz) uncooked noodles per person
- ❑ Dried egg noodles are often packed in layers. As a general rule, allow one layer per person for a main dish
- ❑ If you plan to re-cook the noodles after the initial boiling or soaking – for example, in a stir-fry – it's best to undercook them slightly
- ❑ When cooking a layer, block or nest of noodles, use a pair of forks or chopsticks to untangle the strands from the moment the noodles go into the water

Thai Egg Noodles

Hands-on time: 15 minutes, plus soaking
Cooking time: about 15 minutes

1 lemongrass stalk, inner leaves only, finely chopped

100g (3½oz) medium egg noodles

100g (3½oz) sugarsnap peas, halved diagonally

4 tbsp vegetable oil

4 garlic cloves, crushed

3 large eggs, beaten

juice of 2 lemons

3 tbsp Thai fish sauce

2 tbsp light soy sauce

½ tsp caster sugar

50g (2oz) roasted salted peanuts

½ tsp chilli powder

12 spring onions, roughly chopped

150g (5oz) bean sprouts

2 tbsp freshly chopped coriander, plus extra to garnish

salt and freshly ground black pepper

1. Put the lemongrass in a heatproof bowl with the noodles. Pour over 600ml (1 pint) boiling water and put to one side for 20 minutes, stirring from time to time.

2. Cook the sugarsnap peas in salted boiling water for 1 minute, then drain and plunge them into ice-cold water.

3. Heat the oil in a wok or large frying pan, add the garlic and fry for 30 seconds. Add the beaten eggs and cook gently until lightly scrambled. Add the lemon juice, fish sauce, soy sauce, sugar, peanuts, chilli powder, spring onions and bean sprouts to the eggs. Pour the noodles, lemongrass and soaking liquid into the pan. Bring to the boil and bubble for 4–5 minutes, stirring from time to time.

4. Drain the sugarsnap peas, then add them to the noodle mixture with the chopped coriander. Heat through and season. Garnish with coriander and serve immediately.

Serves 4

Sweet Treats

Make Your Own Ice Cream

Rich and creamy, fresh and fruity or sweet and indulgent, ice creams and iced desserts are easy to make. Good ice cream should have a smooth, creamy texture. Using an ice-cream maker is the best way to achieve it, but freezing and breaking up the ice crystals by hand works well, too.

Vanilla Ice Cream

To serve four to six, you will need:
300ml (½ pint) milk, 1 vanilla pod, split lengthways, 3 medium egg yolks, 75g (3oz) golden caster sugar, 300ml (½ pint) double cream.

1 Put the milk and vanilla pod into a pan and heat slowly until almost boiling. Take off the heat and cool for 20 minutes, then remove the vanilla pod. Whisk the egg yolks and sugar in a large bowl until thick and creamy. Gradually whisk in the milk, then strain back into the pan.

2 Cook over a low heat, stirring with a wooden spoon, until thick enough to coat the back of the spoon – do not boil. Pour into a chilled bowl and leave to cool.

3. Whisk the cream into the custard. Pour into an ice-cream maker and freeze or churn according to the manufacturer's instructions, or make by hand (see below right). Store in a covered freezerproof container for up to two months. Put the ice cream in the fridge for 15–20 minutes before serving to soften slightly.

3

Variations

Fruit Ice Cream: sweeten 300ml (½ pint) fruit purée (such as rhubarb, gooseberry, raspberry or strawberry) to taste, then stir into the cooked custard and churn.

Chocolate Ice Cream: omit the vanilla and add 125g (4oz) plain chocolate to the milk. Heat gently until melted, then bring almost to the boil and proceed to the end of the recipe.

Coffee Ice Cream: omit the vanilla pod and add 150ml (¼ pint) cooled strong coffee to the cooked custard and churn.

Making ice cream by hand

1. If possible, set the freezer to fast-freeze 1 hour ahead. Pour the ice-cream mixture into a shallow freezerproof container, cover and freeze until partially frozen.
2. Spoon into a bowl and mash with a fork to break up the ice crystals. Put back into the container and freeze for 2 hours more. Repeat and freeze for a further 3 hours.

Three-ingredient Strawberry Ice Cream

🍴 **Hands-on time:** 10 minutes

500g (1lb 2oz) hulled and frozen strawberries

75g (3oz) icing sugar

125ml (4fl oz) double cream

1 Put all the ingredients into a food processor. Pulse until the strawberries are fairly broken down, then whiz until the mixture is smooth.

2 Serve immediately or transfer to a freezerproof container and freeze for up to one month. Allow the ice cream to soften a little at room temperature before serving.

SAVE TIME

To get ahead, make this in advance and keep it, well wrapped, in the fridge for up to two weeks.

Perfect Berries

Soft fruits – strawberries, blackberries, raspberries and currants – are generally quick to prepare. Always handle ripe fruits gently as they can be delicate.

Washing berries

Most soft fruits can be washed very gently in cold water. Shop-bought blackberries will usually have the hull removed. If you have picked blackberries yourself the hulls and stalks may still be attached, so pick over the berries carefully and remove any that remain. Raspberries are very delicate, so handle very carefully; remove any stalks and hulls. Leave strawberries whole.

1 Place the berries in a bowl of cold water and allow any small pieces of grit, dust or insects to float out.
2 Transfer the fruit to a colander and rinse gently under fresh running water. Drain well, then leave to drain on kitchen paper.

Hulling strawberries

1 Wash the strawberries gently and dry on kitchen paper. Remove the hull (the centre part that was attached to the plant) from the strawberry using a strawberry huller or a small sharp knife.
2 Put the knife into the small, hard area beneath the green stalk and gently rotate to remove a small, cone-shaped piece.

Perfect Chocolate

Chocolate is a delicious dessert ingredient. It also makes great decoratio
and a simple sauce with many variations. The type of chocolate you choo
will have a dramatic effect on the end product. For the best results, bu
chocolate that has a high proportion of cocoa solids, preferably at least 7

Melting

For cooking or making decorations, chocolate is usually melted first.

1 Break the chocolate into pieces and put in a heatproof bowl or in the top of a double boiler. Set over a pan of gently simmering water.
2 Heat very gently until the chocolate starts to melt, then stir only once or twice until completely melted.

Chocolate sauce

1 Chop plain chocolate (at least 70% cocoa solids) and put it in a pan with 50ml (2fl oz) water per 100g (3½oz) chocolate.
2 Heat slowly, allowing the chocolate to melt, then stir until the sauce is smooth.

Churros with Chocolate Sauce

Hands-on time: 30 minutes
Cooking time: about 25 minutes

200g (7oz) plain flour

150g (5oz) caster sugar

1 tsp baking powder

1½ tbsp olive oil

vegetable oil to deep-fry

1 tsp ground cinnamon

For the chocolate sauce

100g (3½oz) plain chocolate, chopped

1½ tbsp golden syrup

125ml (4fl oz) double cream

1 Put the flour, 60g (2½oz) of caster sugar and the baking powder into a bowl. Stir to combine. Beat in the olive oil and 250ml (8fl oz) freshly boiled water from the kettle. Keep mixing until the dough is combined, warm and sticky. Put to one side.

2 One-third fill a large pan with vegetable oil and heat to 175°C.

3 While the oil is heating, mix the remaining sugar and the cinnamon on a lipped plate.

4 When the oil is ready, fill a piping bag fitted with a 5mm (¼in) star nozzle with dough. Working in batches (about five at a time), carefully squeeze a rough 10cm (4in) length of dough into the hot oil, snipping it off at the nozzle with kitchen scissors. Cook, turning occasionally with a metal slotted spoon, until the churros are golden. Lift out on to a baking sheet lined with kitchen paper, then toss in the sugar mixture and stack on a serving plate. Repeat with the remaining dough.

5 When the last batch of churros is cooking, put all the ingredients for the chocolate sauce into a pan and gently melt together over a low heat. Serve the churros with the warm chocolate sauce.

Strawberry Doughnuts

Hands-on time: 25 minutes, plus rising
Cooking time: 20 minutes, plus cooling

250g (9oz) plain flour, plus extra to dust

1 × 7g sachet fast-action (easy-blend) dried yeast

100g (3½oz) caster sugar

100ml (3½fl oz) milk

25g (1oz) butter

1 medium egg

sunflower oil to fry

175g (6oz) seedless strawberry jam

½ tsp ground cinnamon

1 Put the flour, yeast and half the sugar into a bowl. Heat the milk and butter in a pan until just warm, then tip into a jug and beat in the egg. Pour the liquid into the flour mixture and stir to make soft dough. Tip on to a lightly floured worksurface and knead for 5 minutes until smooth. Put back into the bowl, cover with clingfilm and leave to rise in a warm place for 30–40 minutes.

2 Line a baking sheet with baking parchment and tip the dough on to a lightly floured worksurface. Pat into a rough rectangle 1cm (½in) thick and stamp out 12 rounds with a 5.5cm (2¼in) pastry cutter. Set the rounds on a baking sheet, cover with clingfilm and leave to rise for 20 minutes.

3 Fill a large pan a third full with oil and heat to 150°C. Fry the doughnuts in batches of four until golden brown, about 7 minutes, turning over halfway through. Drain the doughnuts on kitchen paper and cool for 5 minutes.

4 Fit a piping bag with a 5mm (¼in) plain nozzle and fill with jam. Use a skewer to poke a hole into the centre of each doughnut through the side, push in the piping nozzle and squirt in some jam. Mix the remaining sugar and cinnamon and tip on to a plate. Roll the doughnuts in the sugar mixture and serve warm.

Makes 12

163

Perfect Batters

Batters can serve a number of purposes, and are remarkably versatile for something so simple. All you need to remember when working with them is to mix quickly and lightly.

Pancakes

To make eight pancakes, you will need: 125g (4oz) plain flour, a pinch of salt, 1 medium egg, 300ml (½ pint) milk, oil and butter to fry.

1 Sift the flour and salt into a bowl, make a well in the centre and whisk in the egg. Gradually beat in the milk to make a smooth batter, then leave to stand for 20 minutes.
2 Heat a heavy-based frying pan and coat lightly with fat. Pour in a little batter and tilt the pan to coat the bottom thinly and evenly.
3 Cook over a moderately high heat for 1 minute or until golden. Turn over carefully and cook the other side for 30 seconds to 1 minute.

Perfect Zesting

Citrus zest is an important flavouring and is simple to prepare. When using the zest, wash the lemon with a tiny drop of washing up liquid and warm water, then rinse with clean water.

Zesting

1 Wash and thoroughly dry the fruit. Using a vegetable peeler, cut away the zest (the coloured outer layer of skin) taking care to leave behind the bitter white pith. Continue until you have removed as much as you need.
2 Stack the slices of zest on a board and shred or dice as required using a sharp knife.

Easy zesting

To use a zester, press the blade into the citrus skin and run it along the surface to take off long shreds.

To use a grater, rub the fruit over the grater, using a medium pressure to remove the zest without removing any of the white pith.

2

Crêpes Suzette

Hands-on time: 20 minutes, plus standing
Cooking time: 15 minutes

1 quantity crêpe batter (see page 164)
1 tsp golden icing sugar
grated zest of ½ orange
a knob of butter, plus extra to fry
2 tbsp brandy

For the orange sauce

50g (2oz) golden caster sugar
50g (2oz) butter
juice of 2 oranges
grated zest of 1 lemon
3 tbsp Cointreau

1 Flavour the crêpe batter with the icing sugar and orange zest, then leave to stand for 30 minutes. Just before cooking the crêpes, melt the knob of butter and stir it into the batter.

2 To cook the crêpes, heat a small amount of butter in a 15–18cm (6–7in) heavy-based frying pan. Pour in just enough batter to cover the bottom, swirling it to coat. Cook over a medium heat for about 1 minute or until the crêpe is golden underneath. Using a palette knife, flip it over and cook briefly on the other side. Lift on to a plate, cover with greaseproof paper and keep warm while you cook the others in the same way, interleaving each with a square of greaseproof paper to keep them separated.

3 To make the orange sauce, put the sugar into a large heavy-based frying pan and heat gently, shaking the pan occasionally, until the sugar has dissolved and turned golden brown.

Take off the heat and add the butter, orange juice and lemon zest. Put the pan back on to the heat, and stir the sauce until it begins to simmer. Add the Cointreau.

4 Fold each crêpe in half and then in half again. Put all the crêpes back into the pan and simmer for a few minutes to reheat, spooning the sauce over them.

5 To flambé, warm the brandy and pour it over the crêpes. Using a taper and standing well clear, ignite the brandy. When the flame dies down, serve immediately.

Serves 4

Waffles

🍴 **Hands-on time:** 5 minutes
Cooking time: 16 minutes

125g (4oz) self-raising flour

a pinch of salt

1 tbsp caster sugar

1 medium egg, separated

25g (1oz) butter, melted

150ml (¼ pint) milk

½ tsp vanilla flavouring (optional)

butter and golden or maple syrup,
  or vanilla ice cream and fresh fruit
  to serve

1 Heat the waffle iron according to the manufacturer's instructions.

2 Mix the flour, salt and sugar together in a bowl. Add the egg yolk, melted butter, milk and flavouring, if you like, and beat to give a smooth coating batter.

3 Put the egg white into a clean, grease-free bowl and whisk until it forms stiff peaks, then fold into the batter. Pour just enough batter into the iron to run over the surface.

4 Close the iron and cook for 2–3 minutes, turning the iron if using a non-electric type. When the waffle is cooked, it should be golden brown and crisp and easily removed from the iron – if it sticks, cook for a minute longer. Cook the remainder in the same way.

5 Serve immediately with butter and golden or maple syrup. Alternatively, layer the waffles with whipped cream or vanilla ice cream and fresh fruit.

Serves 4

Calorie Gallery

564 cal ♥ 38g protein
g fat (11g sat) ♥ 5g fibre
51g carb ♥ 1.6g salt

per spring roll 235 cals
11g protein ♥ 4g fat
(0.1g sat) ♥ 3g fibre
39g carb ♥ 2.7g salt

18

409 cal ♥ 16g protein
17g fat (2g sat) ♥ 10g fibre
48g carb ♥ 0.8g salt

20

309 cal ♥ 14g protein
4g fat (3g sat) ♥ 11g fibre
51g carb ♥ 3g salt

22

387 cal ♥ 16g protein
g fat (5g sat) ♥ 2g fibre
41g carb ♥ 1.5g salt

per ½ pizza
700 cal ♥ 31g protein
38g fat (17g sat) ♥ 6g fibre
57g carb ♥ 2.6g salt

38

334 cal ♥ 41g protein
7g fat (1g sat) ♥ 2g fibre
27g carb ♥ 0.6g salt

40

395 cal ♥ 12g protein
19g fat (6g sat) ♥ 12g fibre
44g carb ♥ 1.5g salt

42

562 cal ♥ 52g protein
3g fat (2g sat) ♥ 1g fibre
70g carb ♥ 0.5g salt

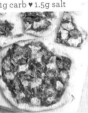

188 cal ♥ 27g protein
3g fat (0.4g sat) ♥ 4g fibre
13g carb ♥ 0.5g salt

60

329 cal ♥ 17g protein
24g fat (14g sat) ♥ 7g fibre
13g carb ♥ 0.7g salt

62

314 cal ♥ 19g protein
8g fat (1g sat) ♥ 21g fibre
44g carb ♥ 3.3g salt

64

298 cal ♥ 22g protein
g fat (4g sat) ♥ 4g fibre
15g carb ♥ 1.4g salt

232 cal ♥ 14g protein
18g fat (4g sat) ♥ 3g fibre
6g carb ♥ 0.9g salt

76

337 cal ♥ 22g protein
20g fat (11g sat) ♥ 5g fibre
17g carb ♥ 0.8g salt

78

286 cal ♥ 12g protein
11g fat (2g sat) ♥ 0.6g fibre
33g carb ♥ 0.8g salt

82

267 cal ♥ 32g protein
13g fat (8g sat) ♥ 0.5g fibre
5g carb ♥ 3.6g salt

84

434 cal ♥ 27g protein
12g fat (2g sat) ♥ 3g fibre
54g carb ♥ 0.5g salt

86

338 cal ♥ 9g protein
27g fat (16g sat) ♥ 5g fibre
19g carb ♥ 0.5g salt

88

431 cal ♥ 12g protein
28g fat (4g sat) ♥ 8g fibre
34g carb ♥ 4.3g salt

90

303 cal ♥ 23g protein
10g fat (2g sat) ♥ 3.5g fibre
32g carb ♥ 0.7g salt

102

524 calories ♥ 23g protein
17g fat (4g sat) ♥ 17g fibre
80g carb ♥ 2.9g salt

104

307 cal ♥ 21g protein
5g fat (1g sat) ♥ 48g carb
16g fibre ♥ 1.7g salt

106

703 cal ♥ 29g protein
24g fat (14g sat) ♥ 5g fibr
102g carb ♥ 1g salt

108

79 cal ♥ 0.5g protein
8g fat (1g sat) ♥ 1g fibre
3g carb ♥ trace salt

124

29 cal ♥ 1g protein
0.3g fat (0.1g sat) ♥ 2g fibre
5g carb ♥ 0.6g salt

126

360 cals ♥ 5g protein
28g fat (16g sat) ♥ 4g fibre
23g carb ♥ 1.2g salt

128

400 cal ♥ 10g protei
20g fat (11g sat) ♥ 2g f
50g carb ♥ 1.6g salt

130

320 cal ♥ 4g protein
13g fat (8g sat) ♥ 0.4g fibre
45g carb ♥ 0.8g salt

144

339 cal ♥ 26gprotein
11g fat (2g sat) ♥ 5g fibre
37g carb ♥ 0.4g salt

146

385 cal ♥ 17g protein
25g fat (4g sat) ♥ 4g fibre
23g carb ♥ 4.9g salt

150

175 cal ♥ 1g protein
11g fat (7g sat) ♥ 0.9g fib
18g carb ♥ 0g salt

156

657 cal ♥ 44g protein
g fat (7g sat) ♥ 10g fibre
50g carb ♥ 3.9g salt

454 cal ♥ 38g protein
31g fat (10g sat) ♥ 0.2g fibre
7g carb ♥ 1.1g salt

448 cal ♥ 20g protein
7g fat (3g sat) ♥ 6g fibre
82g carb ♥ 3g salt

637 calories ♥ 47g protein
39 fat (14g sat) ♥ 2g fibre
24g carb ♥ 3.2g salt

96

98

100

104 cal ♥ 3g protein
g fat (0.4g sat) ♥ 1g fibre
18g carb ♥ 0.2g salt

90 cal ♥ 4g protein
6g fat (1g sat) ♥ 2g fibre
8g carb ♥ 0.3g salt

195 cal ♥ 5g protein
1g fat (0.2g sat) ♥ 1g fibre
34g carb ♥ 0.3g salt

137 calories ♥ 2g protein
13 fat (2g sat) ♥ 3g fibre
2g carb ♥ 0.1g salt

116

118

122

249 cal 9g protein ♥
4g fat (1g sat) 2g fibre
48g carb ♥ ??g salt

per bhaji
87 cals ♥ 2g protein
4g fat (4g sat) ♥ 2g fibre
11g carb ♥ 0.3g salt

450 cal ♥ 7g protein
21g fat (3g sat) ♥ 5g fibre
55g carb ♥ 1.4g salt

202 cal ♥ 3g protein
6g fat (1g sat) ♥ 4g fibre
34g carb ♥ 0.1g salt

136

138

140

226 cal ♥ 2g protein
2g fat (5g sat) ♥ 0.9g fibre
27g carb ♥ 0.1g salt

per doughnut 261 cal
3g protein ♥ 13g fat
(3g sat) ♥ 0.9g fibre
35g carb ♥ 0.1g salt

392 cal ♥ 8g protein
16g fat (9g sat) ♥ 1g fibre
48g carb ♥ 0.4g salt

207 cal ♥ 6g protein
8g fat (4g sat) ♥ 1g fibre
31g carb ♥ 0.8g salt

162

166

168

Index

PICTURE CREDITS

Photographers:
Steve Baxter (pages 7 right, 17, 25 left, 31, 49, 65, 93 right, 99 and 109); Martin Brigdale (pages 51, 53 left, 69, 73, 75, 77, 79, 85, 87, 135 tr, 139, 147 and 151); Nicki Dowey (pages 11, 43, 83, 89, 91, 93 left, 101, 111 left, 123, 125, 131, 145, 153 left and 163; William Lingwood (pages 110, 135 cl and 137); Gareth Morgans (pages 2, 4, 6, 7 left, 9, 15, 19, 21, 23, 24, 25 right, 27, 37, 39, 45, 52, 53 right, 59, 63, 67, 71, 105, 107, 117, 133, 135 br and 157); Myles New (pages 13 and 115); Craig Robertson (pages 32, 33, 44, 46, 56 left, 80, 81, 134, 143, 148, 154–55, 158, 159, 164 and 165); Jon Whitaker (pages 29, 34, 41 and 61); Kate Whitaker (pages 92, 95, 97, 102, 103, 141, 152 and 161); Lucinda Symons (pages 54, 56 right, 111 right, 119, 129, 153 right, 167 and 169); Philip Webb (page 127).

Home Economists:
Anna Burges-Lumsden, Joanna Farrow, Emma Jane Frost, Teresa Goldfinch, Alice Hart, Lucy McKelvie, Kim Morphew, Aya Nishimura, Katie Rogers, Bridget Sargeson, Stella Sargeson, Sarah Tildesley, Kate Trend, Jennifer White, Mari Mereid Williams.

Stylists:
Tamzin Ferdinando, Wei Tang, Sarah Tildesley, Helen Trent, Fanny Ward, Mari Mereid Williams.

BAKE ME A CAKE

There's always time for cake

EASY PEASY MEALS

Easy meals for every day

LET'S DO BRUNCH

Mouth-watering meals to start your day

CHEAP EATS

Budget-busting ideas that won't break the bank

WONDERFUL ONE-POTS

Easy peasy recipes made in just one pot

Available online at store.anovabooks.com and from all good bookshops

SUPER SOUPS

Sumptuous soups for every day

SKINNY SUPPERS

Delicious, nutritious recipes under 300 calories

SLOW STOPPERS

Slow-cooked meals packed with flavour

GREAT VEG

Inspired ideas for delicious veggie meals

AL FRESCO EATS

Easy grills, barbecues and picnics

ROAST IT

There's nothing better than a delicious roast

FLASH IN THE PAN

Spice up your noodles and stir-fries

GLUTEN-FREE AND EASY

Oh-so-good-for-you recipes that taste great

LOW FAT LOW CAL

Nice recipes don't need to be naughty